TO BRUNO

AMF would like to thank all their young members,
whose curiosity and questions have shown them how to write this book.

Concept & scholarly advice
AMF (Amici dei Musei Fiorentini)

Storyline
Simone Frasca

Adaptation
Andrea Paoletti

Texts
Manuela Benedetti, Donata Buttafuoco, Laura Ciuccetti, Diletta Corsini,
Gina La Spina, Gianluca Mengozzi (AMF, Sezione didattica 'G. Mazzoni Rajna');
Monica Fintoni, Simone Frasca, Andrea Paoletti

Illustrations
Simone Frasca and Silvia Vanni

Photographs
Marco Arduino, Franco Casini, Gianluca Mengozzi, Nicolò Orsi Battaglini,
Antonio Quattrone, Archivio Mandragora

Mandragora s.r.l.
via Capo di Mondo 61, 50136 Firenze
www.mandragora.it

English translation
Christina N. Caughlan, Andrea Paoletti, Mark Roberts

Editing, design & typesetting
Monica Fintoni, Andrea Paoletti, Franco Casini

Printed in Italy

ISBN 978-88-7461-384-7

This book is printed on TCF (totally chlorine free) paper.

For information:

AMF

AMICI DEI MUSEI
FIORENTINI

Via degli Alfani, 39
50121 Firenze
☎ 055 286465

FLORENCE

JUST ADD WATER...

Mandragora

SCOURGE

TOURISTS

There are two ways of visiting Florence: you can hire a tourist guide (above, in a 14th-century lozenge-shaped panel from Giotto's Bell Tower); or you can join Philip and Uncle Charlie on their explorations. Well, as Uncle Charlie would say on such (and many other) occasions, "Your move..."

PROLOGUE

here were two versions of the accident. Dad insisted that the root wasn't there the day before: "It popped up during the night! I told you not to plant that laurel by the entrance!" he whined as they helped him into the car. Mum retorted that the he had simply had one beer too many over dinner ("But all those hot peppers, and the spicy salami!" he pleaded, amidst complaints, scrounging for support from his indignant loved ones). The fact remains that his tumble in the garden had cost the architect a fractured leg ("Nothing serious," the doctor had declared, "fifteen days in bed and three months in a cast.") It had also cost the family their eagerly awaited holiday in Egypt. But first things first.

It had all started one Sunday in December, in the best of all possible ways: a light homework load and winter holidays just around the corner. Philip was sprawled on his bed, reading *The Lost Continent* and waiting for the sports broadcast. His mother's voice drifted through the closed door, announcing that Uncle Charlie would be coming to Christmas dinner. Philip left Atlantis to sink on its own and ran into the kitchen to get the details. Uncle Charlie, a.k.a. Professor Charles Hendry, was a famous archaeologist who scoured the world over for traces of lost civilizations. On the rare occasions that he returned home, Philip would stick to him like super-glue, giving him a third degree just short of Inquisition standards. His mother would complain that she never got a chance to talk to her brother ('What could she possibly have to say to him anyway...' Philip wondered), and he was shuffled off to bed. The following morning after breakfast, Philip would start back in with his questions. "What atrocious manners! Is this how I raised you?" Mum would lament. But Charles was fond of his curious nephew, and the truth is that you could really spend hours just listening to his tales.

Anyway, Uncle Charlie made it home for Christmas. When dinner was over, the family got settled in the living room, ready to toast to his latest discovery: a sleepy mummy, perhaps? a deciphered language? an Aztec ball? Uncle Charlie

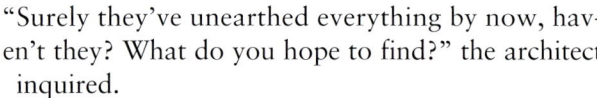

didn't disappoint them: he was excavating in the Valley of Kings, and started talking of papyri and tombs.

"Surely they've unearthed everything by now, haven't they? What do you hope to find?" the architect inquired.

"So what about Carter, mmm?" blurted Philip. "With that attitude he would have never found the *necropolis* of Tutankhamen!" Necropolis: now there was a word that sounded so good he couldn't wait to use it.

No one dared reply, and Philip began to bombard the digger with questions. Charles withstood the deluge bravely, responding with precision and patience—two very essential qualities in his line of work.

While the rest of the family was occupied with their coffee, Philip decided that the moment had come to throw down the gauntlet. "Will you take me on one of your expeditions one day?" he asked Uncle Charlie in a low voice; and with a conspiratorial air he added: "I sure would like to see one of those little temples dedicated to Apopis."

"The jackal?" the architect called from the couch.

"That's *Anubis*, Dad," Philip cut him off impatiently. He turned back to Uncle Charlie with a look as if to say "then the answer is yes?"

"I promise," the archaeologist declared, trying hard not to burst out laughing. "But before we get to travel by ourselves, I believe you'll have company when you come out this summer."

"What do you mean?"

"Ask your parents."

That was how he discovered that even his mother might have interesting news to tell after all.

Everything was ready for their trip to Egypt: the summer had arrived and… thanks to that blessed stumble of his father's, here he was slouching about in his room amidst a pile of books: *The Curse of the Pharaoh, Gods, Graves and Scholars, Watchmen*… Not even the shadow of a pyramid. No sand whatsoever in sight.

He had just got to the good part. The young American photographer, having fled from the courteous but strict observation of the monks, was making his blind way though an underground labyrinth. At the end of a corridor, a torchlight finally

appeared: it was the great hall that held the sarcophagi (another great word!) of the Tibetan priests. Designs of constellations decorated the walls. It was like a voyage in time: the further he went, the more ancient the remains. A strange glow emanated from the last sarcophagus in the line, lost in the shadows: the lid was ajar. The body, perfectly preserved, wore a sort of tunic, and the mouth was replaced by a glowing disc. He was about to touch it when the corpse opened its eyes and... the telephone rang.

Philip just about hit the roof. He flung the book on his bedside table and leaned against the wall to catch his breath.

"No, everything's fine, but you know how he is, always on the move..." his mother was saying. Then a few moments of silence. Then, "Oh, I'm sure he'll be delighted!"

'If it's Aunt Phyllis inviting me to the country cottage, they can just forget about it,' Philip thought to himself. Actually, he always had a good time in the country, but just then, the last thing he needed was a quiet weekend out of town.

"Philip! Uncle Charlie wants to talk to you!"

Philip set the world record for the twelve-metre dash.

"Philip? Can you hear me?"

"Uncle? Hello? Hello! I can't... I can barely hear you. Where are you?"

"I'm on... ile... in Rome... I've got... prop... from the... for the price of one."

"Uncle? I can't hear you! Say that again!"

Uncle Charlie's voice grew clearer. "I was saying, instead of your coming to see me in Egypt, we could get together in a city whe..."

"We got disconnected!" shouted Philip. His mum was at the door. "He'll call back, won't he?"

One ring.

"Where?" he bellowed into the receiver. Maybe the line had fallen again. Maybe it was someone else.

"Have you ever been to Florence?" asked the voice of Uncle Charlie.

ARRIVAL

THE JOURNEY

A couple of days later, the two were on a plane—ETA about 45 minutes.

"So I understand you've got a thing about ancient Egypt."

"I once read that the perimeter of the Cheops pyramid divided by its height is equal to 3.14. And that they found a light bulb on the remains of a ship that sunk a long, long time ago…" And so on, from the Book of the Dead to the astronaut of Palenque. "Speaking of which, how do you explain the fact that during the very same period, different peoples constructed pyramids on both coasts of the Atlantic? They say it has something to do with Atlantis. That's where that god with the beard came from… Quizz… what's his name?"

"Quetzalcoatl. Yeah, he was a character: setting himself on fire and all that… Anyway, if you like mysteries, I'm sure the Etruscans won't disappoint you."

"The Etruscans… The ones that spoke the famous unreadable language!"

"They were the first to settle in Tuscany. In fact, the name Tuscany comes from *Tuscia*: the Romans called it that in honour of its first inhabitants. As for the language… yes, scholars are still trying to *decipher* it properly."

"So did the Etruscans found Florence?"

"No. You see, they preferred to live in the hills, whereas Florence is in the flatlands on the shores of the Arno River. In those days the rivers didn't have artificial banks,

10

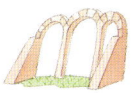
and the plains tended to get pretty marshy. Just imagine: mosquitoes the size of pigeons, malaria spreading like crazy. Plus, the flatlands were more exposed to enemy attacks."

"Right."

"So they settled in the hills, where they founded Fiesole. They were a stone's throw from the river, which was good for commerce, and in the meantime they kept an eye on the Apennine passes connecting the Po Valley with Central Italy. But those were the same reasons that attracted the Romans some centuries later."

"Of course."

"The Romans didn't have any problems founding cities on the flatlands: they were good engineers and knew how to build dikes for the rivers and reclaim the marshes. Look, we're flying over Fiesole now."

"And there's Florence!"

"Exactly. Look at the dome on that cathedral. It's one of the biggest in the world. And there's the Arno River… and that's the Ponte Vecchio. It was built at the narrowest point of the Arno: it may be the very spot where the Etruscans had their port on the river. From up here, if you look closely, you can see the imprint left by the Romans."

"What imprint?"

"You see that big piazza not far from the cathedral square? See how the streets surrounding that square come together at right angles to form a sort of grid? That grid design, like the kind you find on graph paper, tells you that Florence was founded by the Romans. All of their colonies were designed that way."

"But why?"

"Because Piazza della Repubblica, that square near the cathedral, was the centre of the *castrum*, the military camp around which the city was built. It was a rectangle scored by two main streets, the *cardo* and the *decumanus*. These two streets divided the rectangle horizontally and vertically into equal parts: the *cardo* ran north–south, and the *decumanus* east–west. And all of the other streets of the *cas-

trum were parallel to those two: there you have your grid."

"And to defend themselves from their enemies?"

"There were city walls with four big gates: two for the *cardo* and two for the *decumanus*. Can you make out the form of the ancient city now?"

"You're right! It looks like a barbecue grill smack over the centre of Florence."

"Speaking of barbecue, I'm beginning to get a little hungry."

"Me too, but... the other clues?"

"All it'll take is a map of the city and a walk to the centre."

PIAZZALE MICHELANGELO

The archaeologist and his nephew found Giulia waiting for them at the Amerigo Vespucci airport. Giulia was a restorer from the Soprintendenza, and a friend of Charles's. They had met during a conference in Naples, where she had found Uncle Charlie's lecture "stunning—and I really mean it!" Dinner followed, and then a film, then periodic long-distance phone calls and plenty of e-mail. After introductions were made, they launched into the usual chit-chat.

"Well, if this isn't a lovely day we have! And your trip went all right?"

"It was great. We saw the outline of the Roman city. You can only see it from above, like the Nazca designs."

Giulia gave her friend an inquisitive glance. "Are you familiar with *The X-Files*? Mulder and Scully? Amateurs!" he murmured, narrowing his eyes as Philip got in the car. He added: "I'm starving. Let's take a ride up to Fiesole: we'll have lunch in a *trattoria* and spend the afternoon at the theatre." His proposal was unanimously approved.

Giulia had a surprise up her sleeve. "Philip, seeing as this is your first trip to Florence, I've got you a little something. It's in that bag next to you."

"Whatever possessed you, Giulia? You shouldn't have."

"Really, now. It's just a trifle."

Not even mildly interested in these rituals of etiquette, Philip plunged into the bag. Inside there was a piece of paper that, once unscrolled, revealed an antique view of Florence.

Uncle Charlie promptly donned his reading glasses. "It's a reproduction of the *Carta della Catena*, or 'Chain Scroll.' They called it that for the chain

WHEN FLORENCE BECAME THE CAPITAL OF ITALY (IN 1865), IT WAS DECIDED TO GIVE THE CITY A FACE-LIFT: GIUSEPPE POGGI LAID OUT AN IMPRESSIVE RING ROAD AROUND FLORENCE, THE 'VIALI DI CIRCONVALLAZIONE.' ON THE NORTH SIDE OF THE ARNO (THE RIGHT BANK) THIS RING ROAD TOOK THE PLACE OF THE MEDIEVAL WALLS, WHICH WERE PULLED DOWN; ON THE SOUTH SIDE (OR LEFT BANK, WHERE PALAZZO PITTI IS) THE ROAD RAN JUST OUTSIDE THE WALLS, WHICH WERE LEFT STANDING. THE AVENUE WITH ITS PANORAMIC VIEWS, CULMINATING IN PIAZZALE MICHELANGELO, WAS NAMED 'VIALE DEI COLLI,' OR AVENUE OF THE HILLS.

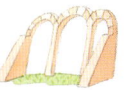

pattern that frames the landscape. Florence as seen from the hills of Bellosguardo... in 1470. When you feel more at home here, you'll enjoy spotting the monuments that were already standing back in those days, like the Palazzo Vecchio, and, well, those that were not."

They were driving along a tree-lined boulevard. Charles looked around, perplexed. "What road are you taking? We're headed..."

"Sorry, but we couldn't do without the obligatory panoramic viewpoint. Come now, Charles, you've even put some weight on."

The avenue opened onto a large square where Giulia, after several fruitless spins, finally wedged her way into a parking space.

"Here we are," sighed Uncle Charlie. "Piazzale Michelangelo."

"The town that you see across from you, over on those two hillsides," continued Giulia, "is Fiesole. And look here below: what a magnificent view."

"Yeah, and lots of tourists, too! I can't believe we managed to park the car."

Philip had been struck momentarily speechless, but, not surprisingly, he didn't stay that way for long. "That big statue in the centre of the square... I can't believe it, it's Michelangelo's *David*! And it's... green?"

"It's just a copy," explained Giulia. "And there are plenty more of those around. But don't worry, you'll get used to them."

A HOP UP TO FIESOLE

Philip had wolfed down a hearty lunch, yet showed no signs of the lethargy that often accompanies the conclusion of a good meal. He launched back into his favourite sport with enthusiasm, resuming his questions in the cool of a pleasant arbour.

"Are there many Etruscan remains in Fiesole?"

"Actually, no—just a stretch of their city walls: and judging from what remains of them, they must have been formidable. But they weren't enough. The Etruscan city was conquered by the Romans, and gradually lost its importance. *Florentia*, in the meantime, just kept growing. That's why you can still identify so much Roman influence in Fiesole, whereas Florence buried its past under squares, avenues and modern architecture. Florence, however, does have the Archaeological Museum, with works of art and household items that date back to the Etruscans. Otherwise you'd have to go and look in another city of the *dodekapolis*."

"*Dode*-what?"

"It's a Greek word," Giulia broke in, "that means 'twelve cities.' The dodekapolis was the confederation of Etruscan cities. Its religious centre was Orvieto."

"But where did the Etruscans come from?"

"Not from outer space, we know that for sure," resumed Uncle Charlie. "It's a difficult subject that has been debated for over two thousand years. The problem is that the Etruscans were very different from their neighbours both in terms of language and tradition. That's why it was thought that they had come from abroad, from the East or the North, and that later, for one reason or another, they had moved to Italy. Others think that they originated here, but simply developed

differently from everyone else. Anyway: for a while they divided the pie with the Greek colonies, from whom they bought vases and precious artefacts. Little by little, they imposed their culture over much of the peninsula, and they even ruled Rome for a while. Then the Romans caught a favourable wind and they, too, started to spread out."

"And at that point the Etruscans just disappeared?"

"Certainly not. They were absorbed by Roman culture, but not without leaving their mark. When it was a question of 'reading' a bolt of lightning, for example, even the Romans relied on Etruscan wisdom."

"I don't believe I caught that: reading a bolt of lightning?"

"According to the Etruscans, the sky was divided into various sectors occupied by supernatural beings. The principal gods lived in the East; the gods of the earth and sky were to the South; the world of the dead and its hellish creatures occupied the West; and the mysterious and powerful gods of destiny lay to the North. All these gods revealed themselves to man through natural phenomena, plants, animals, and so on, because the various subdivisions in the sky were reflected on the earth as if in a mirror. Every single thing, even the most insignificant, could represent an indication of divine will. That's why the Etruscans wouldn't lift a finger without first checking what sort of mood their gods were in. They developed special techniques for interpreting these signs: the so-called art of divination, for which they were famous throughout the ancient world. The most important form of divination was hepatoscopy, that is, the study of the entrails, and particularly the liver, of sacrificed animals. Then came the observation of lightning bolts and of the flight of birds. And, of course, they interpreted prodigious events…"

"Personally, I always liked the Etruscans for their love of dance and music," interrupted Giulia.

"They were obsessed with music. It seems that there was never a moment of peace in Etruscan towns: they were like people today who keep the stereo or television on all of the time. They played music during their boxing matches… who knows, they may have even invented aerobics," Charles teased Giulia, who held physical exercise in the highest regard.

"Why don't we head towards the archaeological zone just behind the cathedral?" she proposed, pretending to have missed the allusion.

15

"Forward, march!" barked Charles, heading resolutely towards the exit. Having forgotten to pay the bill, he was politely brought to attention by the waiter.

"You can catch up with us," remarked Giulia cheerfully, and she turned down a small side street.

For the second time, Philip was rendered speechless. He had expected to see a column or two left standing by some small miracle. Instead, a perfectly preserved Roman theatre loomed behind the entrance gate.

"It's so well-preserved," noted Giulia, as if she had read his mind, "that tonight we can come here for the cinema. The Romans built it during the imperial age. The Etruscans, notwithstanding their love of dance, didn't have permanent theatres."

Philip leapt from one step to the next, incredulous.

"People would bring a snack and a pillow to sit on, just like we do today."

"Did you decide on a film?" asked Uncle Charlie, who had just walked up.

"We were waiting for you," replied Giulia, and headed down towards the orchestra pit.

"But… what if it starts to rain?" asked Philip.

"We'll get wet," observed his uncle, smoothing his beard as he always did when seized by an unpleasant thought. "In order to protect themselves from rain or sun, the Romans covered the *cavea*—the steps, that is—with the *velarium*: great linen tents that were stretched over the public's heads. This place has wonderful acoustics, which is why they hold so many concerts here. Giulia! Say something! Come on!" he shouted in his friend's direction.

The minuscule Giulia shook her blond head no.

"Charles, please!" she could be heard muttering.

"Did you catch that?" exclaimed the archaeologist triumphantly. "And she always talks in such a low voice!"

Giulia was making broad gestures in the direction of the baths. The two swiftly caught up with her.

"As well as those enormous baths that may have served as swimming pools," she began, "you can still see the foundations of what was one time covered over: the *frigidarium*, the *tepidarium* and the *calidarium*. You see, they didn't just go to the baths to get cured, like they do today: it was a gathering place, with amusements and pastimes of every kind. Sure, you bathed, but you could also read, hang out with friends or play sports. It must not have been a particularly tranquil spot: just imagine the hair-raising shrieks, children's squawking and mothers' distracted or anxious calls... Then there were the brawls and the chases after the thief who had stolen your tunic..."

"Sounds contemporary enough," observed Philip.

"You had to pay to get in, of course, but such a small amount that anyone could afford it."

"Here's the *frigidarium*," announced Charles, balancing on a large stone. "It was the cold room: you can recognize it by the three big arches separating it from that room over there, which was a sort of gym. You'd jump into that huge bath of cold water after your work-out. The *tepidarium*, on the other hand, is here to

the right: it was called that because the water, heated by the steam from the *calidarium*, was…"

"Tepid."

"Exactly. See those square openings in the walls of the *tepidarium*? That's where the hot air that circulated under the floor of the *calidarium* entered. There's the floor, held up by small columns. The hot air was generated

in the *praefurnium*, a room with two ovens that you find behind the *calidarium*. Slaves were in charge of heating the water in big pots. The steam, along with smoke from the burning wood, penetrated under the floor through the arch between the oven and the *calidarium*."

"Didn't their feet get roasted?"

"Sandals were hardly invented yesterday."

"Look here," said Giulia, nearing what remained of a wall. "Now it's broken off, but this was one of the hollow bricks that served as a vent for excess steam. Without this emergency valve, the floor would have exploded."

"They had the embarrassment of choice," Uncle Charlie sighed, resting on a low wall. "Where shall I bathe today? In the rectangular pool in front of the oven arch, or in the semicircular one to the right?" He patted his neck dry with a gaudy chequered handkerchief and added: "A problem the barbarians didn't much worry about—they didn't really go in for bathing, you know. During the Middle Ages, this entire area was turned into a cemetery. Or, as I'm sure you'd put it, a necropolis."

"What a sorry end for a place like this…" concluded Philip. "Hey, what sort of tree is that?"

"Time out: no more answers for today," grumbled his uncle, drenched in sweat. There were only two things he hated more than the heat: free jazz and the Caro-Kann Defence.

Piazza del Duomo

The Square

Once again, our hero was caught with his mouth hanging open. They were standing in the Piazza del Duomo, or Cathedral Square, and Philip was having a hard time deciding what to look at next. His rebellious lock of hair—first blocking one monument and then the other—didn't help.

"This piazza is packed with treasures just standing out here in the open," Uncle Charlie admired enviously. "And to think that I have to dig for months just to find an earring!"

"That's the Baptistery of San Giovanni, or St John," Giulia began, "where every child in Florence used to be baptized. Baptism wasn't only important for its religious value: it also served social and registry purposes. It was an opportunity to celebrate the arrival of a new Florentine, and also to record the birth officially. Baptism was a collective ceremony performed only twice a year, but the baptistery was also used for parties and public gatherings. It basically served as a covered town square."

In the meantime, Philip had made up his mind: he looked up.

"Santa Maria del Fiore," Charles informed him, "is the main church in town. That's Giotto's Bell Tower over there, and our old buddy, the Dome. We got a good look at him from the aeroplane, remember?"

"Gigantic," Philip murmured, wishing he could come up with a better adjective.

"That's exactly the way they planned it to be. Even now that Florence is a pretty good-sized city, you can still spot it from miles away. Now where did Giulia run off to?"

"I think I saw her going into the baptistery," Philip replied, and headed off in her direction.

"Couple of things you should know before we go in. The baptistery is, of

course, dedicated to St John the Baptist, patron saint of Florence. Florentines honour St John the Baptist every 24 June, and in the evening they launch a wonderful fireworks display from Piazzale Michelangelo. But from the Middle Ages through the 1500s, the celebration lasted three whole days. Every 22 June, they set up a fair in this very piazza, showing off the finest goods that the city and surrounding countryside had to offer. The booths were protected by colourful curtains, and the entire area between the baptistery and the cathedral—right where we're standing—was covered over with an enormous canvas, embroidered with golden stars. A solemn procession wound its way through each of the city districts, carrying the flags of all the cities under Florentine dominion. At the end of the procession, these flags were put on display…"

THOMAS PATCH,
"SANTA TRINITA BRIDGE AT NIGHT" 20

"In the baptistery."

"Which also happens to be the site of the famous 'explosion of the cart'."

"What's that?"

"It's a sort of fortune-telling ritual that takes place every Easter. The ceremony is very old, apparently dating back as far as the First Crusade—end of the 11th century [Philip was about to ask whether that was B.C. or A.D., but he wisely refrained]. Some 2,500 Florentines participated in the Crusade, including the noble Pazzino de' Pazzi—in Italian, 'Little Nutcase'."

"Nutcase? And I thought Philip was bad!"

"There isn't much to laugh about in the Pazzi family history, I'm afraid, but we'll get to that later. Pazzino, at any rate, got off to a good enough start. It seems that during the Siege on Jerusalem, which was in Muslim hands, Pazzino was the first to scale the city walls. For this remarkable act of courage Pazzino won considerable recognition from Godfrey of Bouillon, leader of the crusading armies. His rewards included three precious chips of stone from the Holy Sepulchre. Pazzino brought them back to Florence, and today they're preserved in the old church of Santi Apostoli. They're nothing more than flints, actually, but they have great historical value: for centuries, the Florentines used them to light the 'Holy Fire' which was distributed, once a year, to every household in the city."

"So what does the cart have to do with it?"

"It was the cart they used to pick up the consecrated fire. The cart's decorations grew more and more elaborate over time, as did the fireworks: as early as the 1400s, people were coming to see them from all over the world. By Pope Leo X's day—that is, the early 1500s—the ceremony unfolded exactly as it does today. Four oxen draw the cart up to the baptistery. An metal wire is run from the cart all the way to the choir of the cathedral. A small dove-shaped rocket is lit and shot down the length of the church nave. When it hits the cart at the other end the fireworks go off, and the square is alive with booms, smoke and sparks. If all goes well and the cart explodes on the first attempt, the harvest will be plentiful."

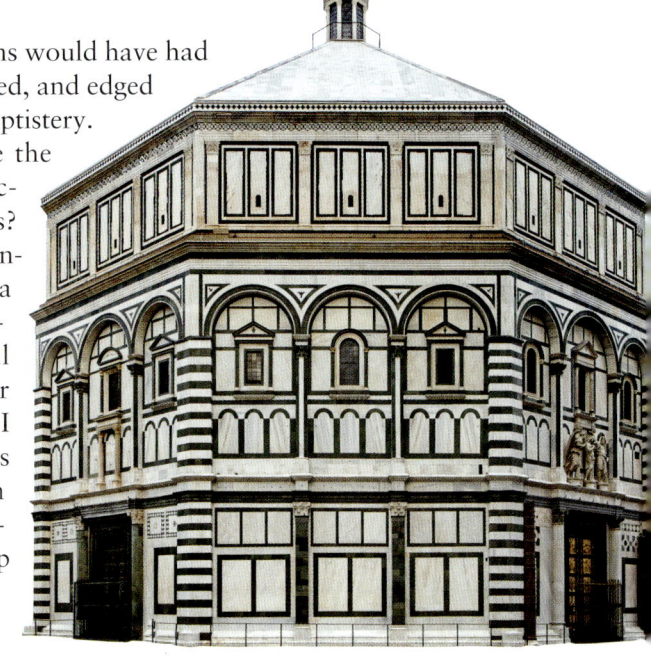

"I wonder what the Etruscans would have had to say about that," Philip mused, and edged towards the entrance of the baptistery.

"One more thing. You see the green-and-white marble facing, with its geometric patterns? That's typical of ancient Florentine architecture. It also had a lot of influence on later buildings, including the cathedral and bell tower. There's another thing I wanted to tell you, but I guess it will have to wait. It has to do with Paradise, and we can look at it after the Last Judgement. Come on, let's catch up with Giulia."

THE BAPTISTERY OF SAN GIOVANNI

Once his eyes were accustomed to the dim lighting, Philip took a look around, and didn't see much to write home about. Then Uncle Charlie put a hand on his shoulder and pointed up to the ceiling: every square inch of the dome was covered with glittering mosaics.

"That's Christ towering there in the middle, looking rather severe. He's deciding the fate of mankind in the Last Judgement. With his open right hand, he welcomes the few elect into Heaven. With his down-turned left hand, he sends the damned to Hell."

"People didn't behave very well around here, did they? Hell is much bigger than Heaven."

"Dante Alighieri would definitely agree with you. Anyway, the depiction of

Hell was supposed to scare people—let them know that saving their souls was no small business. The imagery had to be very clear, because most of the believers didn't know how to read. If you wanted to give importance to something, you had to make it big. They didn't care much about realistic proportions in those days."

"So that's why Christ is so much bigger than the others."

"You got it. The gold background had a special purpose, too: the sparkling reflections are supposed to 'reproduce' the supernatural light of God. So, are you enjoying the cool?"

Giulia had tiptoed up behind them.

23

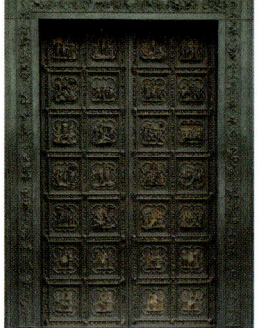

"It's lovely. So what do you think, Philip?"

"Everything still looks a little weird to me."

"That's to be expected," Giulia reassured him. "But you know, these artists weren't at all worried about making their images life-like. The rigid symmetry that you're picking up on, the difference in size between the figures or between certain body parts—it was all planned out that way from the start. Different artists worked on the mosaic designs throughout the 1200s, and styles change a lot over the course of a century. In fact, if you look closely, you'll notice that some of the scenes are much more animated than others: the story comes across better, and the characters are more 'natural,' less 'stiff.' That's exactly the direction painting would take in the centuries that followed."

"In the meantime, let's make our way to Paradise," Uncle Charlie declared gleefully.

The three of them exited and went around to the door of the baptistery that opens onto Piazza del Duomo.

"Michelangelo once said that the door was good enough for Paradise, and ever since then, people have called it the Gates of Paradise. It's actually the second door that Lorenzo Ghiberti created for the baptistery. This is a copy, paid for by a very rich Japanese company. The gilded-bronze original is kept in the Opera del Duomo Museum—the Cathedral Works Museum, that is."

"It reminds me a little of a comic strip… Hey, there's Adam and Eve!"

"Bingo! The panels show stories from the Old Testament. It goes all the way from Adam and Eve to Solomon and the Queen of Sheba. Ghiberti added realistic details to every scene…"

LORENZO GHIBERTI, "THE CREATION & STORIES OF ADAM & EVE"   …& "STORIES OF JOSEPH" (GATES OF PARADISE)

"Sure enough: you can pick out animals, forests, cities... even clouds."

"...and his characters are elegant and fluid. The sculptor modelled them differently according to their distance from the viewer. The ones in the foreground are larger and they seem to come out at you; the ones farther back are smaller, and those in the very background are small and flattened, or *stiacciati*, as they were called in those days. These different layers give the scene a certain..."

"Depth. And it looks more life-like."

"Exactly. We're talking about two hundred years after the baptistery mosaics were finished, and you can see that the way of viewing the world had changed completely."

"So what can you tell me about the Duomo?" Philip prompted, turning his attention to the cathedral.

SANTA MARIA DEL FIORE

"Well, to begin with, the façade that you see is a little more than a hundred years old. The cathedral's first architect, Arnolfo di Cambio, designed a façade, but only built it up to the level of the first register. It was left that way for centuries, until the late 1500s, when they eventually dismantled it."

"What?!"

"That's right. They took down all the marble, statues and mosaics that decorated it, piece by piece. The person responsible for this disaster was Bernardo Buontalenti. He was an excellent architect, but a tad too ambitious. He wanted to rebuild the façade according to his own design, and he managed to wheedle Grand Duke Francesco into destroying the old one. It was all for nought, in the end: a few years later the Grand Duke died, probably poisoned, and people stopped talking about the façade. Or rather, they kept right on talking, and left it at that."

"That reminds me of the new gym they promised to build at my school... How long did it take to build this stuff, anyway?"

"A good long time. It took a lot of work to build a cathedral during the Middle Ages. The guy who set the first stone could reckon that his grand-grand-grand children might see it completed. Or maybe even *their* grandchildren. If everything went smoothly, that is. Whose grandchildren did I say?"

"I get the point. Go on."

ARNOLFO DI CAMBIO

B. BUONTALENTI

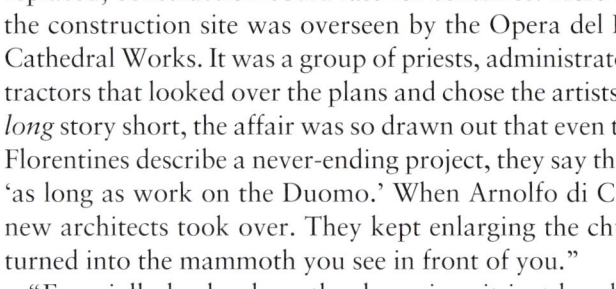

"What with interruptions, doubts, second thoughts and architects replaced, construction could last for centuries. Here in Florence, the construction site was overseen by the Opera del Duomo, the Cathedral Works. It was a group of priests, administrators and contractors that looked over the plans and chose the artists. To make a *long* story short, the affair was so drawn out that even today, when Florentines describe a never-ending project, they say that it's taking 'as long as work on the Duomo.' When Arnolfo di Cambio died, new architects took over. They kept enlarging the church until it turned into the mammoth you see in front of you."

"Especially back where the dome is… it just barely fits in the square."

"Let's take a look inside."

SANTA REPARATA

G.A. DOSIO

Uncle Charlie headed down the nave as soon as they got inside, but Giulia grabbed him by the arm and steered him to the right. There was a small staircase that led down to the crypt.

"Out of my hands," sighed the archaeologist with an air of resignation. "Ready to travel through time? We're about to go down into the oldest church in Florence! After you, mademoiselle."

Giulia turned to Philip. "These ruins are all that remains of Santa Reparata, Florence's first cathedral. It was considered impressive enough when it was built, but towards the mid 1200s, Florence was growing rapidly, and the church was no match for it. So, just to stay on the safe side, they decided to build the biggest church in the world."

GIAMBOLOGNA

"No happy mediums, huh?"

"Not on your life," Charles confirmed. "Florentines were never known for their modesty."

"They got busy on the new cathedral," continued Giulia, "but they couldn't remain without a place of worship. They left Santa Reparata standing, and started to build the new church around the old one. It was sort of like one of those matryoshka dolls: you know, those Russian ones made out of wood that fit one into the oth-

GIOVANNI DE' MEDICI

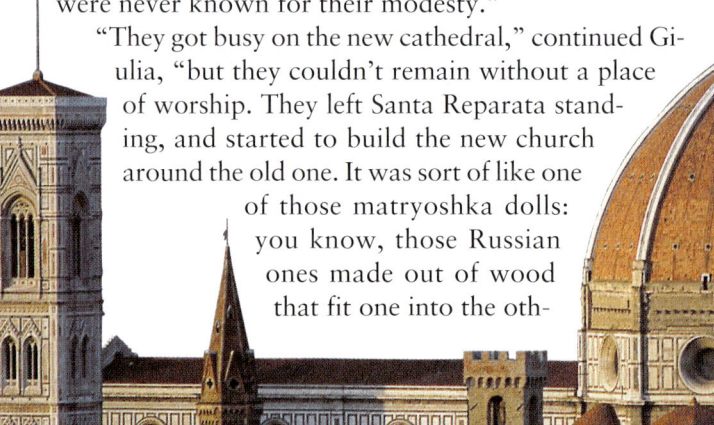

ACCADEMIA DELLE ARTI
DEL DISEGNO

er. Anyway, for over a hundred years they continued to attend services in the old cathedral, more and more suffocated by the walls that were growing up around it. Even though Santa Reparata was condemned, they continued to decorate it and to use it as a burial ground right up to the end of its days."

"This is interesting," Charles cut in. "See those tombstones? A lot of them have the same date: MCCCXLVIII, 1348 in Roman numerals. That was the year of the Black Death: the plague, my dear boy, that spread its lethal way throughout Europe. It hit Turkey, Greece, Spain, France and even London. And Italy, too, of course."

"The plague! I guess a lot of people must have died."

"Look at it this way: in the summer of 1348 alone, the plague killed almost one out of two Florentines. In Europe, it took at least one victim out of three. In his famous *Decameron*, Boccaccio describes the whole thing in gory detail. In fact, the book opens like this: *I say, then, that the years of the beatific incarnation of the Son of God had reached the tale of one thousand three hundred and forty eight, when in the illustrious city of Florence, the fairest of all the cities of Italy, there made its appearance that deadly pestilence.* A chronicler of the time described that *hundreds were dying, day and night, and people fled and abandoned one another, as the disease was spread by breath and vision…*"

"You could catch it just by looking at someone?"

"Of course not. The plague was transmitted by rats and fleas, but no one knew that at the time."

"And just how do *you* keep all this stuff in your head?"

"Actually, I peeked in my guide," Charles confessed. "But I remembered the Boccaccio quotation. You see, I've got a photographic memory."

Philip was willing to let that one slide. "I was wondering… what did the survivors do?"

"They fled from the city, and prayed. The *Decameron*, by the way, is about a group of youngsters who go off into the country to escape the epidemic: they proceed to really live it up in order to forget the horrors they had seen. One of these days I'll bring you to Orsanmichele, where are there are still some reminders of that awful year."

THE CATHEDRAL'S BELL TOWER WAS DESIGNED BY THE FAMOUS PAINTER GIOTTO, WHO WAS ALSO AN ACCOMPLISHED ARCHITECT. HE SUPERVISED CONSTRUCTION ONLY UP TO THE FIRST REGISTER, THOUGH: AFTER HIS DEATH ANDREA PISANO E FRANCESCO TALENTI TOOK OVER. ANDREA ALSO UNDERTOOK THE DECORATION OF ITS BASE: THE HEXAGONAL PANELS WITH THE STORIES OF GENESIS AND THE DISCOVERERS OF THE ARTS ARE MOSTLY HIS WORK (AND HIS SON NINO'S), EXCEPT FIVE, CARVED BY LUCA DELLA ROBBIA. RIGHT ABOVE THE HEXAGONS, A LINE OF LOZENGE-SHAPED PANELS ON A BLUE MAJOLICA BACKGROUND DEPICT THE PLANETS, THE VIRTUES, THE LIBERAL ARTS (YET AGAIN!) AND THE SACRAMENTS. ABOVE THE LOZENGES ARE THE STATUES OF THE PROPHETS. MOST FAMOUS OF ALL IS DONATELLO'S "HABACUC," KNOWN TO FLORENTINES AS 'PUMPKIN-HEAD' FOR HIS BALD, GLOSSY SCALP. BUT WATCH OUT! THE STATUES ARE ALL COPIES: THE ORIGINALS ARE ON DISPLAY AT THE OPERA DEL DUOMO MUSEUM.

PIAZZA DEL DUOMO

WITHOUT FAÇADE!

THREE DESIGNS SUBMITTED

IN THE 19TH-CENTURY, AND

THE TWO MAIN SOLUTIONS:

'BASILICAL'

& 'THREE-POINTED'

Philip was feeling a little queasy after all this plague talk, which, however, didn't spoil his curiosity. "Why does the floor have all these different levels?"

"Every level corresponds to a different epoch. You can walk along an early Christian mosaic, then turn to your right along the brick-laid level; climb up a step and there's a colourful mosaic from the Charlemagne period, and so forth. Look, there's a tombstone that still has some of its colour. In the Middle Ages it was fairly common to paint the tombs."

"The display cases hold objects they found in the graves," Giulia explained. "A knight's sword, a Lombard glass, a scalpel…"

"Before we go back up," Charles suggested, "I want to show you one last tombstone. They found it during excavations in 1972."

Philip painstakingly read the epitaph out loud: "*Corpus magni ingenii viri Philippi Brunelleschi Florentini*. That's Latin."

"Bravo! It says, 'Here lies Filippo Brunelleschi, a Florentine of great genius'."

"What did he do that was so special?"

"You can see for yourself when we go upstairs. Come on."

INSIDE THE DUOMO

Back at the surface, Philip had the same impression as when he first entered: from the inside the Duomo looked like a big empty box, decorated here and there with faded colours. All in all, it was a let-down after the fabulous exterior. He mentioned this to his uncle.

"There's actually quite a lot of art in here, from the frescoes to the stained-glass windows: it's the sheer vastness of the place that gives you that impression."

"It's so huge that everything else seems minuscule."

"The so-called 'Gothic effect' brings the viewer's eye upwards: the soaring piers, the lancet arches…"

"Those are the pointy ones, right?"

"Yes. You see, this type of arch is able to bear a lot more weight than the 'rounded' arch: this allowed architects to construct enormous cathedrals, all of them straining towards the heavens. Then there was the religious sentiment of the time —mankind was considered small and insignificant compared with its Creator. Anyway, here in Italy, Gothic architecture generally remained pretty toned down and 'classic:' a question of differing tastes and influences. If you like 'pointy' architecture, you should see what the French were able to come up with!"

Philip looked around. "Why don't those two knights have haloes? They look more like warriors than saints."

29

"In fact, they weren't saints at all. They were mercenary captains. The frescoes show two equestrian monuments seen in perspective, from the bottom up. One is supposed to be marble, and the other—the greenish one—bronze. These guys were paid to fight, and they won some important battles for Florence. That's why it was decided to honour them here in the city's most sacred spot."

"How about that clock?" Philip gestured up at the interior façade. "I've never seen the likes of it."

"It was painted by Paolo Uccello, the artist who did the green knight. By the way, *uccello* means 'bird' in Italian."

"Bird, Nutcase—what was wrong with these people?"

"Some of those were actually nicknames, like you might call one of your classmates Beanpole or Butterball. His real name was Paolo di Dono. According to Vasari, they called him Uccello because he loved animals, but couldn't afford to have one. He had to content himself with painting them, and the walls of his house were apparently covered with dogs, cats and birds! Others think they started calling him that when Ghiberti won the competition to decorate the baptistery's North Door. Paolo was one of the apprentices in Ghiberti's studio, and he was stuck with the job of doing all the animals and birds for the friezes. That may be why…"

"So then what happened?"

"He signed up with the Physicians' and Apothecaries' Guild, which was the official corporation artists went into—can you believe *that*? From there, he went on to the Company of St Luke, which was the association specifically for painters. He went to Venice at a certain point and learned to do mosaics: unfortunately, none of the work he did there survived. When he returned to Florence, the Cathedral Works commissioned this fresco. The knight is John Hawkwood, or Giovanni Acuto as they call him around these parts, an English mercenary who fought for Florence for almost twenty years."

GIOVANNI ACUTO

Niccolò da Tolentino

"It looks just like a real statue…"

"That's because Paolo used perspective. Still there are some peculiarities. The pedestal is seen from below, for example, while the horse and knight are at eye-level. The horse's body is actually just a series of different-sized circles placed next to each other. Vasari thought it was odd that the horse was seen walking with both of his left hooves on the ground at the same time… Anyway, Paolo was a strange sort of fellow."

"Why do you say that?"

"At a certain point, he developed a genuine obsession with perspective, and would stay up all night long drawing wine glasses and hats and whatnot. His wife would call him to bed, and he would just keep repeating, *Oh, what a sweet, sweet thing is this perspective!*"

"He lost his marbles!"

"He was definitely into it, and apparently didn't do much of anything else. He would close himself indoors for months and refuse to see anyone… But Paolo's perspective wasn't the artificial, mathematical one that Brunelleschi used: it was a 'natural' perspective that tried to reproduce the way we actually see things. He deliberately experimented with a series of 'mistaken' effects: optical illusions, double perspective, mirrors… Many centuries later, the Cubists and Surrealists would play with these very elements, exploiting Paolo's imaginative legacy."

Philip looked up with renewed curiosity: "The clock we saw isn't exactly normal-looking either."

"The clock face is a daisy with twenty-four petals, one for each hour of the day and night. The only hand is in the shape of a shooting star, and moves anticlockwise. It doesn't even tell the right time! Back then, the day started just after dusk, with the first hour of night. The next day started the following evening. The hand moves anticlockwise because it follows the movement of the shadow cast by the sun, from East to West, like a sundial."

"Incredible. Even Swatch hasn't come up with that."

"I wouldn't be so sure… And speaking of trademarks, there on the floor is a big OPA monogram—the abbreviation for Opera, the Cathedral Works."

Giulia felt obliged to add her piece. "The floor is inlaid with marble of different colours to

form geometric patterns. With each panel, the intarsia form a sort of spider web of perspective: if you stood in the middle where the sign of the Opera is, you'd feel like you were about to get swallowed up!"

INTARSIA COMES FROM THE ARAB 'TARSÌ,' MEANING PRECIOUS DECORATION: AND IN FACT THEY WERE MADE WITH VALUABLE WOODS, MARBLES OR OTHER STONE. FLOORS WERE MADE OF SLABS OF DIFFERENTLY COLOURED MARBLES, SAWN WITH METAL SAWS AND THEN POLISHED WITH POWDERS OF TUFA OR PUMICE. THE INDIVIDUAL PIECES WERE CUT OUT INTO THE EXACT SHAPES REQUIRED BY THE DESIGN. THE NATURAL GRADATIONS OF COLOUR WERE CLEVERLY EXPLOITED.

BRUNELLESCHI'S DOME (THE CUPOLA)

Philip looked directly above him. "It's enormous. Who could have done that?"

"Who, but a man of great genius?"

"Filippo Brunelleschi!"

"You got it. And just imagine: it would seem even bigger if they had left it all white, instead of frescoing it with all those angels, devils and saints."

"Tell me all about it."

"The Dome has a strange history of arguments, rivalry and cock-eyed schemes. But mostly it's the story of the architect who designed it: a courageous man, and a genius. At the end of the 1300s, the Florentines decided to cap off their cathedral with a truly enviable dome. It was a matter of prestige, you know. Two hundred years earlier the detested Pisans had designed their so-called 'Piazza of Miracles,' with its Leaning Tower. Florentines were not be outdone: they would settle for nothing less than the world's Eighth Wonder. So they called in Arnolfo di Cambio to oversee the project: he was one of the most famous architects of the day. Now, when they went about building a church, they usually started with the apse. Instead, Arnolfo started from the front, and being a good sculptor as well, he even made some of the statues for the façade. But here's the catch: he never explained how they were supposed to build the dome he had designed. The architects who came in after him didn't know where to begin, and they frankly did their damnedest to avoid the issue altogether. The cathedral itself was finished in the early 1400s, but there was still no dome in sight. So the city held another competition to decide who would get to construct it. They had loads of proposals—and let me tell you, some of them were downright absurd."

GIORGIO VASARI & FEDERICO ZUCCARI, "THE LAST JUDGEMENT"
FRESCOES OF THE DOME (GO GRAB YOUR MAGNIFYING GLASS!)

"For example?"

"Catch this. The problem: how could the workers build at that height? Wooden scaffolding cost too much, and there was far too much space to cover. Vasari tells us that there was this guy who proposed filling the drum of the dome up with soil, gradually adding more the higher the dome got. But that presented a fresh problem: how would they empty the church of all that soil once the dome was in place? His solution was original, to say the least: mix a few gold pieces in with the soil. Who wouldn't grab their wheelbarrow at the prospect of a tidy little fortune?"

"Let me guess: he didn't win the competition."

"Clearly not. It ended in a tie between two architects and sculptors, Ghiberti and Brunelleschi. Actually, the design for the dome was 100% Brunelleschi's, but the folks at the Cathedral Works… let's just say they didn't trust him."

"How come?"

"According to Vasari, they thought he was a little crazy. It was the first time anyone had claimed to be able to put up a dome of those dimensions without support scaffolding. They asked Ghiberti to work alongside him, just to keep him in line: he had backing on the commission, and a fine artist he was, too. But there was bad blood between the two men: they argued continuously about how the work should proceed, and construction was moving at a snail's pace. Brunelleschi also happened to be fiercely jealous of his ideas. When he was studying different construction techniques, he would make his models using bricks carved out of turnips: when he was finished, he would cook himself a vegetable soup thus leaving no evidence behind to copy. Eventually Ghiberti turned his full attention to the baptistery doors, and Brunelleschi was free to proceed."

"So what was the problem?"

"The problem was finding a way to hold the dome up while it was under construction, and Brunelleschi devised a brilliant solution. At the beginning of the 1400s, he and Donatello had gone to Rome to study the monuments and sculptures left behind by the ancient Romans. Filippo borrowed one of their methods: he would lay the bricks in an interlocking, herring-bone pattern:

"A MOST IMPOSING STRUCTURE, TOWERING ABOVE THE SKIES,
AMPLE ENOUGH TO COVER WITH ITS SHADOW ALL THE PEOPLES OF TUSCANY"

(LEON BATTISTA ALBERTI)

that way, they wouldn't be able to fall during the mortaring process, even if they were on an incline."

"That little door there leads to a stairway you can follow all the way to the top," Giulia remarked. "It runs up the hollow space in the wall that Brunelleschi left to lighten the structure. When you reach the top, you can go out onto the white marble lantern. Brunelleschi designed that too. Not only it served to illumi-

34

nate the church, but also to fix the dome in place, the same way a keystone fixes an arch. You can see the whole city from up there."

"It must have taken a long time," Philip mused out loud, looking up.

"They had lots of setbacks," Uncle Charlie agreed, "many of which sprang from the rocky relationship between Filippo and Lorenzo. At a certain point, things got so tense between them that Brunelleschi fell back on the age-old strategy of passive resistance. Probably a little like you do when you want to stay home from school."

"I would *never* do that," Philip defended himself casually. 'Even if I wanted to, I'd never get away with it,' he added to himself. His mum was such a worrier that she'd call the doctor at the least little thing.

"He'd pretend he was sick," ('Right,' thought Philip) "and wait for the problems to arise. He wanted everyone to realize that without him, the work would grind to a halt. And that invariably proved to be the case."

The three walked under the large octagonal marble choir, towards the huge piers that bear the weight of the dome.

TWO SACRISTIES

Two sacristies were carved out of the space between the piers. The Canons' Sacristy was closed off by a dark door. The inside of the Mass Sacristy was visible through a stained-glass window. It was all done in wood, and fairly small. There was a table in the middle where things for the Mass were laid out. The room was lined with chests of drawers, and wood inlay on the walls reproduced cabinets full of books, crosses and candelabras.

"Amazing! It's so realistic!"

"I know: the wonders of perspective never cease," Uncle Charlie declared. "When there wasn't enough space, you just had to make it up."

Giulia chuckled knowingly and adjusted her glasses. "This sacristy has seen a thing or two in its time. That business in 1478, for example: now *there* was a thing to remember."

"What happened?"

"It was Easter Sunday. Picture this: a wounded man, running for his life, seeks shelter in this very sacristy. But the thugs want blood, and keep up the pursuit. Just like in the movies. The man was none other than Lorenzo de' Medici, trying to escape the hired daggers of the Pazzi."

"Little Nutcase's relations!"

"Descendants, rather. Pazzino had been dead a long while when all this happened, but his family had grown very powerful in the meantime. Powerful enough to challenge the Medici."

"But Lorenzo de' Medici was the ruler of Florence."

"To all extents and purposes, yes. Together with his brother, Giuliano."

"And the Pazzi decided to bump him off?"

"Exactly. But first they had to come up with some allies, some accomplices. So Francesco de' Pazzi and his father, Jacopo, got the bishop of Pisa involved and even, so it seems, the pope. They decided to attack in the cathedral, during the Easter Mass. Lorenzo and Giuliano were following the service from the choir loft, where the clergy sat along with members of the most prestigious Florentine families. Just when the Host was being raised and everyone was supposed to kneel and bow their heads, boom! The attack. Giuliano died on the spot, his head split open with an axe. Lorenzo fought to free himself from the killers. A friend of his tried to shield him with his own body, and was stabbed to death. Lorenzo, wounded in the neck, managed to leap out of the choir. He and a few friends were able to barricade themselves in the Mass Sacristy—right in there."

"And then?"

"The conspiracy had failed, revenge followed. The Pazzi and their accomplices were slaughtered. Francesco de' Pazzi and the bishop of Pisa were hanged, their corpses strung up outside the Palazzo Vecchio. Jacopo was massacred and tossed into the Arno River. The other conspirators were hacked to pieces, or else joined Francesco and the bishop outside the windows of the Palazzo Vecchio."

All of a sudden the sacristy had taken on very sinister overtones. "Unbelievable. Not exactly subtle, were they?"

"Straight out of a horror flick," Uncle Charlie confirmed. He had enjoyed the bloody tale in silence. "Giuliano's skull is on display at the Anthropological Museum. You can still see the axe mark. Right—after all this gory talk, I think we all need a bit of sunshine… and *gelato*."

GIULIANO DA MAIANO & WORKSHOP, "ANNUNCIATION" (MASS SACRISTY). THESE STUNNING EXAMPLES OF INTARSIA WERE MADE WITH DIFFERENT KINDS OF WOOD: BOX, YEW, WALNUT, CYPRESS… NOT TO MENTION EVEN MORE VALUABLE ONES SUCH AS EBONY, WHICH WERE SPECIALLY IMPORTED FROM THE EAST. SOMETIMES, TO ADD TOUCHES OF LIGHT, OTHER MATERIALS WERE USED TOGETHER WITH THE WOODS: SEMI-PRECIOUS STONES, IVORY, BONE, MOTHER-OF-PEARL.

It wasn't hard to find a *gelateria* near the cathedral. The hard part was choosing between the thirty different flavours.

"Artichoke flavour? Parmesan cheese?" suggested Uncle Charlie.

"Give it a rest… So what's that? What does Buontalenti have to do with it?"

"Our good friend Bernardo—you remember him from the façade. He happened to figure out how to keep ice cream from spoiling. Strongly recommended."

"Now there's a real genius. Almost up to Brunelleschi's standards!"

The three were strolling lazily down Via Calzaioli, cones in hand.

"Know what we're gonna do now?"

Philip and Giulia gave Charles the famous 'whatever-you-have-in-mind-the-answer-is-no' look.

"We haven't finished the cathedral," he retorted indignantly. "I'm bringing you up to the top of the dome."

A look of terror flashed across Giulia's face. "Not on your life, buddy," she answered diplomatically. "I'll wait for you down here. You guys go right ahead."

Philip gave her a wistful look, and resigned himself to the inevitable.

The Dome (with a Vengeance)

It was suffocatingly hot, the stairway seemingly going on forever. And Uncle Charlie was always twenty steps ahead, looking fresh as a rose. "Must have trained on the pyramids," Philip muttered crossly. A doorway at the top led them outside. Below them—a long way down—they could see the entire city of Florence, and beyond.

The lifeless body of Bernardo Bandini Baroncelli in a drawing by Leonardo da Vinci

"Did you count the steps, Philip?" Uncle Charlie was chipper. "There are 463 of them."

"I noticed," Philip panted. "I must be… a little out of… shape."

"Well, go on. Take a seat and feast your eyes."

Twenty minutes later, the tireless archaeologist launched a new attack. "So this afternoon, I was thinking… we might as well pay a visit to the Opera del Duomo Museum: what do you say?"

The two of them were having lunch in a crowded pizzeria in San Lorenzo. Giulia had declined their insistent invitations: she had to go check her e-mail.

"I feel like I already know those Cathedral Works folks. Is it far from here?"

"Just around the corner, in Piazza del Duomo. But if you're not up to it…"

"Who, me? When the going gets tough…"

DONATELLO

THE OPERA DEL DUOMO MUSEUM

"The wonderful thing about this museum," Charles began, "is that it displays all the statues, paintings and tapestries that have been removed from the cathedral throughout the ages. The Florentines wanted an extraordinary cathedral: they weren't kidding around when they said they wanted the grandest in the world. They continued to decorate, update and change it right up to the end of the 1800s. By then, artistic tastes had changed and the 'clean look' prevailed."

"It prevails at my place once a week."

"But I don't imagine you empty your house out. The cathedral, on the other hand, was gradually 'tidied' of all the decorations that had been added over the centuries. Take these two marble singing-galleries. They were originally hung in the cathedral to serve as balconies for the choir to stand in. They've been here since 1688, the year Ferdinando de' Medici got married to Violante of Bavaria. It seems that, according to the prince, they didn't go well with the Baroque decorations in the church."

Luca della Robbia

"There's no accounting for taste. Still, they don't look like garbage material to me."

"They used to be located right above the two sacristy doors, and were both sculpted in the early 1400s: one by the great Donatello and the other by Luca della Robbia. The theme is the same, but the artists took very different approaches to it according to their temperaments. Luca's is very graceful: the singing children are beautiful and the whole thing makes you think of slow, sweet music. Donatello's little angels, in contrast, seem to be in almost frenzied motion. You see the glass mosaics covering the columns and the background in the bas-reliefs? Donatello added those to attract light, knowing that his singing-gallery would be hung in a dark location."

"Who's that over there? Some kind of witch?"

"That's Donatello's extraordinary carving of the penitent *Mary Magdalen*."

"She gives me the creeps. What's she made of?"

"Wood, plaster, oakum… He thought those materials would best render the saint's suffering. See those pinched features? Anyway, she's in good company: all of the statues suffered terribly when they were kept outside."

"What are you talking about?"

"The heat, the cold, the vibrations… not to mention pollution and the pigeons' little offerings. The museum was built on what used to be the yard where they kept statues destined for the cathedral. Now it's the opposite: the statues were removed from the exterior of the cathedral and the bell tower so they wouldn't get ruined. They all live here now. That silver altar, on the other hand, used to be in the baptistery, along with lots of other sacred objects. You know how you can tell them from those coming from the cathedral?"

WOOL GUILD

MERCHANTS' GUILD

ASTRONO

HUNTING

TECHNOLOGY

"There must be a logo or something."

"The sponsor's trademark. That eagle with the bundle of wool in his talons is the emblem of the Merchants' Guild—the Calimala."

"So who sponsored the cathedral?"

"The wealthy Wool Guild. You can see their emblem embroidered on that cloth: the lamb with a halo and a standard between its hooves. You know, the silver altar was solemnly displayed only once a year, on St John the Baptist's Day. They would set it up in the centre of the baptistery, above the ancient baptismal font. It spent the rest of the year disassembled in a cupboard. They used some 400 kilos of silver to tell the saint's story."

"Is it old?"

"It was started during the second half of the 1300s. Florence was particularly rich and powerful in those days, and they had just conquered Pisa. Business was good, the future was looking bright, people were sweating their shirts off. Here, have a look at the original panels from the bell tower—we saw the copies out on the square. The hexagons represent almost every human activity imaginable: *Agriculture*, *Navigation*, *Metalwork*, *Sculpture*, *Weaving*... You can even see the tools and instruments they used back then."

"They certainly look busy."

Uncle and nephew found themselves in a long, well-lit passageway with walls of glass.

"I bet you're going to like this: an entire section dedicated to the construction of the dome! There are tools, devices, models... and Brunelleschi's death mask."

Philip browsed about, absent-mindedly tugging on his lock of hair. "Where did they get the stone blocks from? And how did they drag them up to the dome?"

"First things first. Though architects designed the projects, it was generally the foremen who organized the work and supervised the workers. A building's foundation was usually celebrated in a special ceremony: the cornerstone was laid in the presence of the most important people in the city. The stones themselves came mostly from quarries in Trassinaia, near Fiesole. They were hauled to the construction yard by mules or oxen. The stonecutters would then carve the stones according to their destination: arch, vault, etc. They made their cement by boiling down limestone, and adding water and sand. Then they'd beef up the concoction by adding some hair, cow blood or even earwax."

"Some recipe!"

"But wait, it was still missing the chef's magic touch: generous helpings of garlic (which, by the way, made for excellent glue) so that the devil wouldn't come along and bring the whole thing crumbling down! Anyway, the work wasn't all done by hand. There were machines to lift and position the stones; but since they didn't have either steam power or electricity, the machines were fuelled by animals. Some of the equipment is preserved here: pulleys, iron squares, thick cables for hoisting materials up... There were also some strange devices, like this little cart that would be sent down the ribs of the dome to refresh the workers' brick supply, or these winches and pinchers that were used to lift the blocks of marble or stone. And here are the moulds of the corner bricks devised by Brunelleschi."

AMONG THE STATUES SCULPTED BY ARNOLFO DI CAMBIO FOR THE CATHEDRAL FAÇADE, THIS "VIRGIN WITH THE CHILD JESUS" IS THE MOST... ORIGINAL: HER EYES ARE MADE OF GLASS, A FEATURE THAT IS QUITE UNIQUE IN FLORENTINE SCULPTURE. IT SEEMS THAT BERNARDO BUONTALENTI, THE ARCHITECT WHO TALKED THE GRAND DUKE INTO DEMOLISHING THE MEDIEVAL FAÇADE, NEVER PARTICULARLY LIKED IT: HE USED TO SAY THAT THE GLASS EYES MADE HER LOOK WEIRD, IF NOT DOWNRIGHT UGLY, AND HAD THE STATUE MOVED INSIDE THE CHURCH— WHENCE THOSE VERY EYES KEPT ON WEAVING THEIR SPELL ON EVER-GROWING CROWDS OF PILGRIMS, WHO WOULD COVER HUGE DISTANCES TO VENERATE THE SACRED IMAGE. ANXIOUS FOR THE STATUE NOT TO BECOME THE OBJECT OF POPULAR SUPERSTITION, THE PRIESTS REMOVED IT FROM THE CATHEDRAL AND TUCKED IT AWAY IN THE OPERA'S COURTYARD.

Philip, however, was distracted by the wooden models.

"The models helped him convince his 'client' that it would be possible to build the dome. It worked out for him, this time."

"Why this time?"

"In 1401 a competition was held to determine who would get to decorate the North Door of the baptistery. Brunelleschi submitted the *Sacrifice of Isaac* panel that's kept today in the Bargello. Unfortunately for him, Ghiberti won the competition. Our friend Filippo was very bitter about it, and decided to devote himself to architecture full time. One could certainly say he made the right choice, even though he was a pretty good sculptor."

The collection also comprised a number of rather weird-looking artefacts.

FILIPPO BRUNELLESCHI

LORENZO GHIBERTI

42

"Reliquaries," Uncle Charlie revealed. "You see, once upon a time a church's prestige depended on which and how many relics it could brag about. Take this one, for instance…"

Philip was having a hard time keeping on his feet, and there was a dazed look on his face.

"Are you all right?"

"Not enough to face the relics… Let's take a break."

"I get carried away sometimes, I suppose," Charles apologized humbly. "Let's go back to the hotel. We'll get rested up and catch that Bruce Willis movie this evening. We'll see if we can drag Giulia along."

Philip rolled his eyes. "She probably goes for those sappy love stories…"

"Are you kidding? *I* like those. Giulia won't watch anything but action."

LEFT, MICHELANGELO'S "BANDINI PIETÀ": IT OWES ITS NAME TO THE SCULPTOR FRANCESCO BANDINI, WHO BROUGHT IT WITH HIM TO ROME. MICHELANGELO SCULPTED AT LEAST THREE VERSIONS OF THIS SACRED THEME—THE "VATICAN" (THE ONLY ONE HE ACTUALLY FINISHED), THE "BANDINI" (THIS ONE) AND THE "RONDANINI" (NOW IN THE CASTELLO SFORZESCO, MILAN)—WHEREAS THE "PALESTRINA PIETÀ," ON DISPLAY AT THE ACCADEMIA GALLERY, IS PROBABLY NOT BY HIM. HE MEANT TO USE THE "BANDINI" FOR HIS OWN FUNERARY MONUMENT. THEN, ONE DAY, PERHAPS NOT SATISFIED WITH THE OUTCOME, HE SNATCHED UP A HAMMER AND BEGAN HITTING IT IN A RAGE, SWEARING NEVER TO FINISH IT. THE STATUE HAS LONG BEEN HOUSED IN THE CHURCH OF SAN LORENZO; THEN IT WAS MOVED TO THE DUOMO (HENCE THE NAME OF "PIETÀ DEL DUOMO").

MOSAIC-WORK

MOSAIC-WORK IS A SPECIAL KIND OF DECO-RATION FOR WALLS AND FLOORS. IT WAS USED BY THE GREEKS (WHO ACTUALLY INVENTED THE TINY GLASS CUBES) AND BY THE ROMANS (WHO WERE THE FIRST TO MAKE USE OF GOLD), AND ENJOYED ITS MOMENT OF GREATEST GLORY UN-DER THE BYZANTINE EMPIRE—THAT IS TO SAY THE EASTERN ROMAN EMPIRE—FROM THE 4TH CENTURY A.D. LET'S TAKE A LOOK AT THE TECH-NIQUE.

THE MOSAIC-MAKERS BEGAN WITH A DRAW-ING. HAVING TRACED THE OUTLINE OF THE FIGURES, THEY BEGAN 'FILLING' THEM IN WITH TINY PIECES SET CLOSE TOGETHER. THESE PEB-BLES MIGHT BE OF STONE OR MARBLE ('TAS-SELLI'), OR OF GLASS COLOURED WITH METAL OXIDE ('TESSERAE'). GOLD AND SILVER WERE NEVER MIXED WITH THE GLASS: INSTEAD, A VERY THIN LEAF OF PRECIOUS METAL WAS SANDWICHED BETWEEN TWO TRANSPARENT SQUARES, LIKE A SLICE OF HAM BETWEEN TWO PIECES OF BREAD.

TO MAKE THE 'TESSERAE', WHICH WERE USUALLY SQUARE OR TRIANGULAR, SHEETS OF COLOURED GLASS WERE CHOPPED UP WITH RED-HOT PINCERS. THE INDIVIDUAL PIECES WERE THEN PRESSED INTO A LAYER OF FRESH LIME, PLASTER OR CHALK.

THERE WERE VARIOUS TRICKS TO MAKE THE MOSAIC GLEAM AND GLITTER: FOR EXAMPLE, THE 'TESSERAE' WERE USUALLY SET AT SLIGHT-LY DIFFERENT ANGLES SO THAT EACH OF THEM WOULD REFLECT THE LIGHT IN ITS OWN UNIQUE WAY. GILDED GLASS WAS USED FOR THE SAINTS' HALOES.

IF YOU ARE INTERESTED IN GLASS-PASTE MO-SAICS, BEST SUITED TO WALL DECORATION, WE SUGGEST YOU VISIT THE BAPTISTERY AND THE CHURCH OF SAN MINIATO.

STAINED GLASS

WHY IS THERE SO MUCH STAINED GLASS IN GOTHIC CHURCHES? BECAUSE THANKS TO THE POINTED ARCH AND THE BUTTRESSES, WHICH CAN SUPPORT GREAT WEIGHTS, THERE WAS NO LONGER ANY NEED TO BUILD THE MASSIVE THICK WALLS WE FIND IN ROMANESQUE ARCHITECTURE: GOTHIC WALLS WERE HIGHER AND SLIMMER, THEIR WEIGHT 'LIGHTENED' BY LARGE WINDOWS FILLED WITH STAINED GLASS.

THE WINDOW-MAKERS BEGAN WITH A LARGE DRAWING, IN ONE-TO-ONE SCALE (IN OTHER WORDS, THE SAME SIZE AS THE WINDOW ITSELF), AND, OF COURSE, A SUPPLY OF PIECES OF DIFFERENT COLOURED GLASS.

THESE WERE MADE IN VARIOUS WAYS. COLOURED DYES COULD BE MIXED WITH THE MOLTEN GLASS; THIN PIECES OF DIFFERENT-COLOURED GLASS COULD BE PUT ONE ON TOP OF THE OTHER, SO AS TO OBTAIN THE DESIRED SHADE; OR ELSE DESIGNS COULD ALSO BE PAINTED DIRECTLY ONTO PLAIN GLASS.

USING THE DRAWING AS A PATTERN, INDIVIDUAL PIECES OF GLASS WERE CUT TO THE SIZE AND SHAPE THAT WERE NEEDED. AT FIRST RED-HOT METAL CUTTERS WERE USED, BUT LATER THE WORK WAS DONE WITH DIAMONDS, WHICH GAVE MUCH NEATER AND MORE REGULAR EDGES.

THE INDIVIDUAL PIECES OF GLASS WERE FIXED TOGETHER BY A FRAMEWORK OF LEAD STRIPS. THE STAINED-GLASS WINDOW WAS THEN READY. FLOODED WITH SUNLIGHT, ITS COLOURS WOULD GLOW MOST BEAUTIFULLY—TO EVERYBODY'S DELIGHT.

LORENZO GHIBERTI

PAOLO UCCELLO

DONATELLO

ROMANS & CO

FLORENTIA

he next morning, Uncle Charlie announced that they were headed to *Florentia*. Philip followed him docilely to the Piazza della Repubblica, where they found Giulia engrossed in a French fashion magazine.

"Ready?" Uncle Charlie asked in a sly sort of voice. "Welcome to Florentia!" Philip looked around expectantly, but he didn't see much of anything besides streetlights, cafe tables, parked taxicabs and a fair amount of large buildings.

"Not around you! *Underneath* you! Florentia is three or four metres under our feet. We're walking on it."

"Oh yeah, now I remember. The cardo, the decumanus… This must be the piazza of the castrum where Florence was born!"

"The white marble forum was located here," explained Giulia, "with its *Campidoglio*, or Capitol, and various annexes. The Capitol was the temple dedicated to Rome's three principal gods—Jupiter, Juno and Minerva—and every Roman colony had one. Its ruins are buried under that portico over there, below the Gambrinus theatre. It's no coincidence that the adjacent street is called Via del Campidoglio."

"What about the column in the middle there?"

"That's Roman, too. It marks the spot where the cardo met the decumanus. The statue at the top may well represent the goddess Flora, who Florentia was named after. She was the goddess of vegetation, and the Romans were very fond of her. They honoured her with special circus tricks and other festivals. Via Calimala was the ancient cardo. If you follow it all the

ARCHAEOLOGICAL MUSEUM

way you come to Via Calimaruzza, where underneath the first palace on the right you can visit the remains of the ancient southern city gate. They found some fascinating things under the Piazza della Signoria, too: the ruins of a *fullonica*, for example, where they washed, refined and dyed their fabrics. It's proof that the textile industry in Florence, for which the city would later become famous all over the world, dates back to Roman times. They also found some of the finest baths in all of…"

"Like the one we saw in Fiesole?"

"Even better. Florentia had three, great big ones. Then there was the theatre, of course, five times larger than Fiesole's. Part of Palazzo Vecchio was built right on top of the ancient theatre steps. That's why Via de' Gondi, the road along the building's right-hand side, slopes downhill. The amphitheatre, on the other hand, was outside the city walls, in what used to be countryside not far from the church of Santa Croce. The ground floor is buried, but some of the archways from the first floor can still be seen in Piazza de' Peruzzi. From above, you can reconstruct the am-phitheatre's shape just by following the line of the houses."

"OK, but this is Virtual Florentia. I was hoping to actually *see* something."

"That's why they made the Archaeological Museum."

ARCHAEOLOGICAL MUSEUM

Philip wouldn't have minded a moment or two just to soak it all in, but Giulia promptly dragged him off to look at the Etruscan jewellery. "Seeing as Virtual Florentia disappointed you, we'll have to resort to some special effects."

At first, Philip wasn't particularly impressed. Then, on closer inspection, he realized that the gold had been worked into incredibly fine threads and almost microscopic spheres. "Pretty cool," he conceded.

"Take a look at this sarcophagus. That's Larthia Seanti, stretched out on her banqueting couch. She's got five rings on that one hand alone! You can still see some colour on her sarcophagus, which is unusual: the colours usually fade away altogether with time."

Philip took advantage of the situation to show off a little: "Did the Etruscans take household things with them into the afterlife the same way ancient Egyptians did?"

"Yes. But they thought that the deceased lingered in the grave as a 'presence' or spirit. That's why their tombs looked a little like your typical house, with clothes, decorations and household items, as you said."

"That explains the furniture, and the things to eat and drink," Philip concluded, satisfied.

"It was only later, thanks to Greek influence, that they started believing in an actual afterworld. The Etruscan 'land of the dead' was in-fested with monstrous demons: Tuchulcha, for example, with his hooked nose, mule ears and snakes in the place of hair."

"And what happened to people on the Other Side?"

"The shadows of the dead arrived after a long jour-ney, and remained there for eternity. Everyone was condemned to the same cruel fate, with demons perpetually at their throats."

"No way to get around it?"

"Of course not. In the end, the outlook was too grim, and they realized it. During the last phase of Etruscan civilization, there was a movement that promised a more welcoming afterlife: certain secret rites were supposed to bring a few fortunate elect into communion with the god Fufluns. It was said to guarantee a better fate in the afterworld."

Philip mulled over the kingdom of the dead and its demons, wandering distractedly from one display case to the next. At a certain point, a vaguely alarming statue caught his attention: an animal with the body of a lion, the tail of a serpent and a goat's head on its back. "Now what the heck is this… thing?" he blurted out in amazement.

"A most unlikely sort of beast," Uncle Charlie replied, tired of his long, obedient silence. "So improbable, in fact, that its name has become synonymous with anything that cannot exist in the real world: the *Chimaera*! It was a fire-breathing monster, and only the Greek hero Bellerophon was eventually able to kill it. It seems that the goddess Athena was kind enough to lend him her winged horse, Pegasus, for the occasion."

"The sculpture was unearthed near Arezzo in 1553," continued Giulia, "and caused quite a sensation in artistic circles—among its greatest admirers were the painter Giorgio Vasari and the sculptor Benvenuto Cellini. It's made out of bronze, a material that the Etruscans really knew how to work. Now, here: in addition to a large number of bronze votive statues…"

"Votive?"

"Offerings to the gods. They're easy to identify because they usually represent people in the act of giving something—to the gods, naturally. In addition to these statues, I was saying, the museum has two very large bronzes. We just saw the *Chimaera*. The other is that one over

49

there: the man in the toga, with his arm outstretched as if to silence a crowd. He's called the *Orator*: he's wearing the toga and sandals typical of Roman fashion, but he was actually Etruscan—a 'Romanized' Etruscan, if you like. His name is etched on the hem of the toga: Aulus Metellus. He probably had eyeballs, too, originally."

"They must have got lost…"

"Or else stolen along the way: they were probably made from expensive materials, like ivory or something. The display cases hold some of those famous household items we were talking about. But of course not everyone could afford precious metals or expensive Greek vases like the ones up there on the top level."

"Where do the vases come from?"

"They were found in Etruscan tombs, mostly. Wealthy Etruscans would buy them off Greek merchants and bring them out on special occasions—especially banquets. Now *here's* a real beauty."

They were looking at a large vase decorated with innumerable black figures.

"This is the François Vase," explained Giulia. "It's what we call a 'krater,' deriving from the Greek verb *kerànnumi* that means 'to mix.' In fact, the vase was a sort of centrepiece used to mix wine and water before serving it to the guests. That's why the vase was so important during banquets: its quality was an indicator of how rich the host happened to be."

"This guy must have been a real Bill Gates."

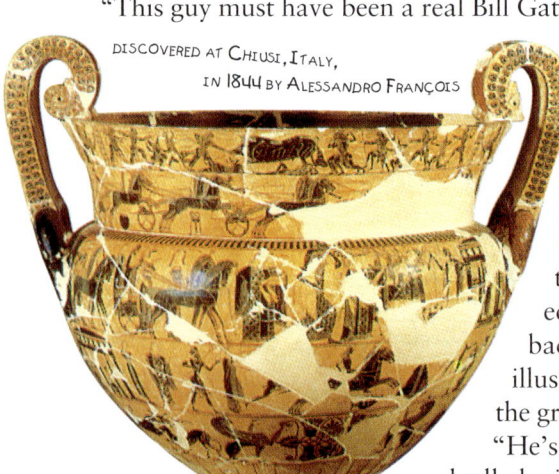

DISCOVERED AT CHIUSI, ITALY, IN 1844 BY ALESSANDRO FRANÇOIS

"No doubt. The potter and the painter both signed it here, see: 'Ergotimos made me, and Kleitias decorated me.' The figures are black on a red background, according to the ancient technique. Later, they changed method and started putting red figures on a black background. This particular vase illustrates the mythological story of the great hero Achilles."

"He's the one with the bum heel, who duelled with Hector, right?"

RED-FIGURE HYDRIA (A WATER-JUG, FROM THE GREEK 'HYDOR', WATER), A MASTERPIECE BY THE PAINTER OF MEIDIAS (5TH CENTURY B.C.)

"The very same. But there are lots of other characters, and they're conveniently identified, too. Here you see Achilles' parents, Peleus and Thetis, getting married. Near the chariot is the name of 'Zeus,' the king of the gods—right there in front of your nose! And to think that this was made 570 years before the birth of Christ: almost a hundred years before the Persian Wars!"

"That's enough vases for one day," the archaeologist interrupted. "Let's go to Egypt!"

Philip was in seventh heaven. A parade of mummies passed before his eager eyes, along with sundry things that had been excavated from the tombs. There were chairs and headrests (wooden half-moons that the Egyptians used as pillows), sandals, musical instruments, figurines and tombstones.

"This is the cream of the crop," Charles admired, pointing to a perfectly preserved wooden chariot. "They used six different types of wood to build this puppy: of course, there wasn't much wood in Egypt, so they had to bring it in from abroad. The rich owner, accompanied by his charioteer, probably used it to go hunting or off to battle. He must have been so proud of it."

"I can imagine. Just like people today cruising around in their Porsche or Ferrari…"

GUELPHS: FROM WELFEN, THE FAMILY OF BAVARIAN DUKES WHO STRUGGLED FOR THE IMPERIAL THRONE IN THE 12TH AND 13TH CENTURY. IN ITALY THEY WERE THE PARTY WHO SUPPORTED THE POPE (AGAINST THE EMPEROR). AFTER 1266 THEY BECAME KNOWN IN FLORENCE AS 'THE BLACKS.'

GHIBELLINES: FROM WAIBLINGEN, THE NAME OF A CASTLE BELONGING TO THE HOHENSTAUFEN, DUKES OF SWABIA, THE ENEMIES OF THE WELFEN. IN ITALY THEY TOOK THE PART OF THE EMPEROR (AGAINST THE POPE). AFTER 1266 THEY BECAME KNOWN IN FLORENCE AS 'THE WHITES.'

MIDDLE AGES & THEREABOUTS

TOWER-HOUSES

Would you like to hear what happened to Florentia some centuries after our Roman friends were out of the picture, during the dark years of the Middle Ages?"

"That's what I'm here for," Philip replied accomodatingly.

"We'll take a stroll around the tower-house city," continued Uncle Charlie, trotting down the hotel stairs, "even though technically speaking, it's not there anymore."

"This isn't going to be another one of your 'virtual tours,' is it?"

"Not exactly. Around the year 1000, when Florence was still quite small, Countess Matilda had a circuit of walls built to protect the city. A few decades later, they were already bulging at the seams. The population was growing fast, small industry was operating at full steam and was exporting wool abroad. Besides which, the Florentines were big fighters: they waged war on each and every neighbouring village. Whenever they conquered one, their inhabitants came to work in Florence. They lacked the money to build a new ring of walls, so they squeezed as much as they could into the existing ones. They made the streets even narrower, orchards and gardens disappeared… They couldn't build out, so they built *up*, and the city gradually filled with towers. A person arriving in Florence back then would see this tall ring of crenellated walls enclosing some two hundred towers, church steeples and the white roof of the baptistery. San Gimignano, between Florence and Siena, still has something of that look."

53

"Sort of like a medieval Manhattan."

"Sort of. Here we are: our tour begins in Via delle Oche, just around the corner from the cathedral. This is the Visdomini Tower, a little fortress they retreated to when enemies attacked. The towers used to be twice as tall as they are today, and there was a crenellated terrace up on top…"

"…that they used to dump boiling oil down on their enemies!"

"Even a rock or two would do. You know, a stone dropped from 60 metres above… Every noble family had its own little private fortress. The Florentines of the time were a bloody lot—they had family feuds that lasted about 150 years."

"How did they start?"

"They're said to stem back to a wedding that was supposed to happen in 1216 and… didn't. The families of the bride and groom got into a spat not far from the Ponte Vecchio, and the head of one of the households was killed. The event had a snowball effect, and Florentines split into various groups, all fighting for control of the city. Later, most people sided with one of two main factions: the Guelphs, who were allied with the Pope; and the Ghibellines, who backed the Emperor. The conflict between popes and

emperors—and between the families who supported either side—lasted for centuries. The popes eventually got the upper hand, and with them, the Florentine Guelphs."

While Uncle Charlie was busy reliving the Dark Ages, the two had reached Piazza Sant'Elisabetta.

"This is the Pagliazza Tower, built out of stone and brick. You'll notice that it's got an elliptical base instead of the square one we saw on the Visdomini Tower. It's also much older, dating back to the Byzantine Age. For a long time, the tower housed an all-women's prison. Unlike male inmates, who had to sleep on the floor of their cells, the women got to sleep on mattresses made out of straw—in Italian, *paglia*: that's where the tower gets its name. Now look down the little alleyway: you see the overhang on the tower down there, braced by the slanting wooden beams? That's called an architectural

'projection,' in this case an enclosed wooden balcony that allowed them to take the best advantage of what little space they had. The technique is used in modern architecture, too, though the walls are usually made out of glass instead of wood. The stone blocks that stick out from the façade of medieval buildings once supported projections. That's what they leaned out of to throw rocks at their enemies, or to dump their waste out into the street… and I mean *any* kind of waste!"

"Are you saying they didn't have toilets?"

"In their dreams! The streets back then were open sewers, unpaved, with a ditch that ran down the centre. The ditches were supposed to channel the rainwater, but they were inevitably clogged with all manner of trash. Plus, all the overhangs blocked the sunlight, so the streets never completely dried out. They must have been a muddy mess."

"I suppose people in the Middle Ages didn't take too many strolls around town."

"*And* there was always the danger of being assaulted by some rival family. In order to defend themselves better, various allied families—*consorterie*, or factions—would build their houses clustered together in small groups. The city blocks were formed by these clusters of houses. You left your block at your own risk."

"Just like pioneers used to put their covered wagons in a circle to defend themselves from the Indians…"

"Florentines of the Middle Ages spent most of their time in the court: not the castle court, with its princes and jesters, but in the courtyard nestled in the centre of the block."

The two made their way down Via del Corso. Passing under a small archway—formerly a city gate patrolled by soldiers—they found themselves in Piazza dei Donati.

"This is typical of Florence: the square was named after the most important family of the *consorteria* that lived there. Here's one of the courtyards we were just talking about. Picture what it must have been like back then, with little kids chasing geese around the well… From the year 1000 until the 1200s, day-to-day life in Florence unfolded in places like this. There's the Donati Tower, just off the square."

"Some tower! Must be fifteen metres high!"

"Towers were averaging about sixty metres in those days. But at the end of the 1200s, in an effort to discourage fighting among the rival factions the authorities decided to knock all the city's private towers down to the height of twenty-five metres. The tower of the city hall was the only one left intact, a symbol of restored law and order. It looks like they got a little carried away with the Donati Tower. Anyway… here's another tower with a rather peculiar history— the *Castagna* or 'Chestnut' Tower. This was the first government seat in Florence: the *priori*—the priors—met here until the end of the 1200s, when a new Priors' Palace—the one known today as Palazzo Vecchio—was built. They call it the Chestnut Tower because of this one time when the priors were under attack by an angry mob. They apparently ran out of stones to throw, and started lobbing down sacks full of chestnuts instead. See those three doorways outlined on the façade? They used to open onto those projections we were talking about. They incorporated an existing tower-house, too, when they were building the palace of the People's Captain in Via del Proconsolo. The tower was converted into the public bell tower: in case of enemy attack or other emergencies, the citizens were summoned by ringing the bell. In the 1500s this palace became headquarters for the chief of police, the *bargello*. That's how the building got the name by which it's still known today."

"What's in there now?"

"Now it houses a museum, but it wasn't a very nice place back then— especially not for people having troubles with the law! In addition to police headquarters, the building served as the city courthouse and prison. The faces of escaped convicts were painted on the building's façade so that people would watch out for them."

"Wanted… dead or alive."

"There were also torture chambers, with a whole collection of atrocious machines and devices… Fortunately, the story has a happy ending. Grand Duke Peter Leopold of Habsburg-Lorraine—the first sovereign in the world to outlaw the death penalty—had the whole arsenal burned in the palace courtyard."

"Civilization triumphs! This calls for a celebration. How about a *gelato*?"

56

PALAZZO DAVANZATI

"So tell me," Philip resumed, cone in hand, "what were these tower-houses like inside? For example, where did they store the ammunition to dump on their enemies?"

Uncle Charlie led him to the entrance of an attractive old building. "This is the museum of the Ancient Florentine Home, perhaps better known as Palazzo Davanzati. This is where you can see how rich families lived in the 1300s and 1400s. The house originally belonged to the Davizzi, then the Davanzati family lived here from the 1500s through the 1800s. It was then bought by an antiquarian who transformed it into a museum, furnishing it with period pieces and household goods. The original things were all lost."

"But is this a tower-house?"

"Palazzo Davanzati has more comforts than most tower-houses, but the defence system is the same, also because the political climate was pretty dicey at the time it was built. From those trapdoors on the ceiling of the loggia they would bomb down stones, garbage and other nasty stuff on the heads of their ill-wishers. Today, the loggia is closed off with wooden portals, but it used to be open to the street and set up as a shop—the owners were wool merchants."

"Weren't they afraid of night raids?"

"Yes. That's why the door leading into the interior courtyard was closed and patrolled every evening, and only trusted friends were allowed inside. This wood-and-stone staircase leads to the upper floors where the bedrooms are located. Before the skylight was put in, both sun and rainwater would enter through that opening."

"I see they had a well, too."

"It was an incredible luxury in those days. Usually they just collected rainwater or took what they needed from the river. Here's the pulley system they used to bring water up to each floor. It runs all the way to the fourth level where the kitchen was located."

"Why so high?"

"For safety reasons. Fires usually started in the kitchen: if this were on the ground floor, rising flames could burn the whole

house down. This way, the damage was limited to the top floor. This big room here on the first floor is the family room. It's the most comfortable, well-lit and spacious room in the house. That niche between the windows is where they stored the rocks that would be launched down through the trapdoors—here they are, on the floor. We saw them from below."

"What a cosy picture: mum making dinner upstairs, granny dropping rocks on somebody's head…"

"Well, a little progress has been made. We don't even use guard dogs anymore: it's all electric fences, photoelectric cells… Almost all of the rooms have handy built-in closets that were completely hidden by curtains hung from the walls. The curtains were colourful and lined with fur. They're known as *capoletti*…"

"Fur-lined? Must have been cold in here… They could have done what Kubrick did—you know, guy who directed *2001: A Space Odyssey*? He moved into a house where there wasn't any central heating, so he bought robes for all his guests to wear."

"Where do you come up with these things? At any rate, yes—the cold *was* a problem. Here's a nice fireplace in the dining room. The wall-hangings were painted with red and blue diamonds and parrot designs. Like I said, they draped the walls with curtains in those days to help keep the heat in."

"With those parrots and everything, they could just sit here and dream of warmer climates."

"Now, there's a fascinating hypothesis— we could write an article or two about it… In the meantime, let's go see where our family *really* dreamed."

A canopy bed was waiting for

them in the bedroom on the second floor.

"Now this is just the bed here, but you'll see the complete room in a fresco by Ghirlandaio in Santa Maria Novella. In the scene depicting the birth of the Virgin Mary, you'll see that they used to place the mattress on top of a broad wooden footboard. It served as a bed, bedside table, bench and wardrobe all in one."

"I'll bet it was more comfortable than the bed in the hotel," Philip noted grumpily, having slept poorly the last couple of nights.

"The bed may have been comfortable, but life was *not*—not for women, anyway."

"Why not?"

"Well, they hardly ever left the house. They spent their time indoors, spinning wool and sewing. Winters were even rougher. Instead of glass, the windows had makeshift panes of canvas or wooden shutters, and you can imagine what kind of cold they let in. Folks just had to make do with warming pans and fireplaces."

"What do you say we take a little walk in the sunshine?"

"Good idea. Off we go to San Miniato."

The Church of San Miniato al Monte

"So who was this San Miniato?" Philip asked as the bus was climbing the Viale dei Colli.

"St Minias, the first evangelist and Christian martyr in Florence. He lived in the 3rd century under the Roman emperor Decius. He was apparently a wealthy Armenian merchant who was decapitated for his faith. According to legend, he picked up his head, which they had just chopped off, and put it back on his neck, then walked off to die in the grotto where he had lived his last years as a hermit."

"And that's where they built the church."

"And the oratory, exactly. This basilica is one of the best-preserved medieval buildings in the city. The façade is inlaid with white marble from the Apuan Alps and green marble from Prato. Does it remind you of anything?"

"The baptistery."

"So you do listen to me when I talk!" Uncle Charlie beamed.

"No, I just happen to have a photographic memory," Philip chided snippily.

"Got me!" gasped Uncle Charlie, clutching his chest as if struck to the heart. "As a matter of fact, all you need to do is look carefully. Let's say you wanted to draw the exterior of San Miniato. You'd realize—actually, I'm sure you already have—that it's really quite simple. All you have to do is follow the green marble strips on the façade and the whole thing breaks down into geometric shapes. This marvellous clarity of form and design lies at the very heart of Florentine artistic

expression: you can find it in art, fashion, literature…"

"And that eagle at the top of the façade?"

"There's one inside the church as well. Since your photographic memory seems to be slipping, allow me to remind you: that's the logo of the Arte di Calimala, the ancient guild of Florentine merchants."

"Oh, yeah! And in the eagle's talons there's this… parcel."

"The *torsello* was a kind of sack they used during the Middle Ages. They would fill it with fabric and miscellaneous merchandise and strap it onto their donkeys. Churches cost a lot of money to build, and they were usually financed by civic organizations, rather than individuals. They would put their emblem up in a prominent place as a good form of advertising."

AROUND CHRIST ARE THE SYMBOLS OF THE FOUR EVANGELISTS

THE EAGLE OF ST JOHN
THE LION OF ST MARK
THE ANGEL OF ST MATTHEW
THE OX OF ST LUKE

THE INTERIOR

The sunlight outside was blinding, and it took their eyes a while to adjust to the church's semi-darkness. They were greeted by an enormous image of Christ wearing a stern expression on his face. The figure sparkled with light.

"A mosaic!"

"And very ancient too, made with gilded tiles. Christ is shown with the Madonna and St Minias, the fellow holding the crown. This must have been a pretty intimidating place for the medieval folk who came here. Christ in the apse dominates the entire nave: it's impossible to miss him. The monks would sit up there on that platform, hidden from the eyes of the congregation. There, in a precious marble enclosure, the services were held. And still are."

"That glass gives the place such an eerie light," Philip observed, gesturing toward the narrow windows of the nave.

"Actually it's not glass at all, but thin slabs of alabaster, a translucent stone that comes from Volterra."

Philip looked around him. "Those designs on the pavement… are astrological signs! What are they doing here?"

"That's the Zodiac. During the Middle Ages, they had the habit of recycling—shall we say—pagan symbols, giving them new meanings: the twelve apostles, the months of the year, the parts of the body… Let's see if we can find our signs. Here we are. That sea goat is Capricorn, and those are the twins of Gemini: a man and woman in medieval clothing."

They climbed the stairway that leads to the upper level of the church.

"Here's the pulpit," Uncle Charlie explained, indicating a small marble terrace surmounted by an imposing lectern. "This is where the priests gave their sermons and explained the Bible to their flock."

"In Latin?"

"No. They used common language that everyone could understand. Come, let's take a look at the crypt. The bones of the martyr are kept in that little stone casket." Charles indicated the altar at the end of the crypt. "Some of his friends

The Roman walls, built after the founding of the city in 59 B.C., traced a rectangle bounded by Piazza del Duomo, Piazza San Firenze, Piazza Santa Trinita and Via Cerretani. But things change. By the 6th century the Western Empire had fallen, the Eastern Empire was tottering, barbarians were on the rampage and the inhabitants (perhaps one thousand in all?) were too few to be able to defend the old circuit; so they built a much smaller one (the Byzantine wall). Later the population increased, and the Carolingian circuit (9th to 10th century) followed the old Roman one, except that it was somewhat enlarged along the Arno. In 1079 the Matildine wall (named after Matilda, Countess of Canossa) included Piazza del Duomo. With the fifth circuit (1172-1175) the enlargement of Florence began in earnest, since many of the houses were by then outside the gates: the new walls were three times as long as the earlier ones, and for the first time they enclosed an area on the south side of the Arno. The sixth and final circuit (1284-1333) coincided with the present 'viale,' or ring road. In the 14th century Florence was becoming a real metropolis, and the city government decided to build really extensive walls, once and for all—much too extensive, as shortly afterwards (in 1348) the Black Death carried off two thirds of the city population.

who suffered similar persecution are in there too. The little columns supporting the vault are made from different types and shapes of marble, because they come from Roman buildings torn down during the Middle Ages."

"They recycled those, too?"

"Yes, but not only for practicality's sake. In medieval symbolism the columns represented the Christians that founded and maintain the Church—not only the building itself, that is, but the entire spiritual community. Also, the recycled columns symbolize the passage from paganism to Christianity."

The Walls & Fort

"So those are the medieval walls?" Philip asked when the two were back outside.

"That's right. They climb up to Fort Belvedere: this is one of the few remaining stretches. During the 1800s, when Florence became the capital of Italy, most of the walls were torn down to make way for boulevards like the one in front of us."

"Battles, charges, cannons… that's the kind of stuff I'm interested in. What can you tell me about the walls?"

"During the Middle Ages and Renaissance, all major cities were surrounded by walls. During the siege on Florence, they needed a way to protect the city from

southern attacks. None other than the great Michelangelo himself transformed the hill on which San Miniato stands into a fortress: the church bell tower was stocked with cannons, and padded with mattresses from top to bottom."

"So that the guards would be more comfortable."

"Very funny. Cannonballs were solid stone, in those days: they weren't explosive. The harder they hit, the more damage they caused. But, of course, they sort of bounced off of the mattresses."

"Like a rubber wall."

"Right. Let's start down now."

Uncle and nephew descended the stairway on Via del Monte alle Croci. They reached an intersection at Porta San Miniato: a steep road to the left led along the fortress walls.

"Wanna go for it?" Philip asked. "It doesn't look that steep."

"Try hiking it under the midday sun and you'll sing a different tune." Uncle Charlie had the knowing voice of someone who had been there. "This is the stretch of wall that we saw from above. These tall, straight city walls were a little like tower-houses as far as resistance was concerned. The defenders would lean out from the crenels and dump down whatever they could find to keep their enemies from scaling the wall. When there was a battle on the horizon, they would put up their bartisans, which were wooden turrets that allowed them to tower over the assailants."

It was a stiff walk up the hill, but the scenery was lovely. It didn't take them long to reach Porta San Giorgio.

"This is the oldest city gate in Florence."

"You can... still see... the hinges," Philip panted, trying hard to conceal his huffing and puffing.

"And the mammoth in front of you is Fort Belvedere."

"Hmm... the walls here are slanted. Easier to attack, perhaps?"

"Wrong! When cannons started showing up on the battlefield, they realized that the old medieval walls, tall and slender as they were, made easier targets. Every cannonball that reached its mark would leave a gaping hole, and the debris would rain down on the

people inside. That's why ramparts were invented: thick, low walls that were slanted to deflect the shells. The architect who designed the fort, Buontalenti, was an expert in fortifications and boundary walls: he built them all over Tuscany."

"He was the ice cream guy, wasn't he?"

"The very same. But he had another speciality, too. On summer evenings, he would shoot off his own home-made fireworks from the fortress battlements.

They were so beautiful they nick-named him 'Bernardo of the Pin-wheels!' Let's go inside and take a rest. And... don't worry—it's a short climb."

Philip shot him a dirty look, but cheered up almost immediately: a large field spread out before them, the very spot from which Ber-nardo had launched his fireworks.

People were stretched out reading or sunbathing on the grass, and the entire city of Florence could be seen in the background. It looked so close you could almost touch it.

'*Belvedere* means nice view in Italian... now I get it...' Philip thought drowsily before following his uncle's example. Charles was already snoring quietly on the lawn.

PIAZZA DELLA SIGNORIA

HISTORY & ARCHITECTURE

hilip's unseasonable craving for hot chocolate and whipped cream was more than satisfied at Rivoire's. He was bursting with energy, and felt like the brawny protagonist in *Doom*—or the computer game of your choice—freshly recharged with a good medicine kit or two. Health: 123%. Side effects: questions, questions and more questions. Uncle Charlie was seated next to him trying to read the newspaper. The Piazza della Signoria stretched out in front of them, overshadowed by the bulky mass of Palazzo Vecchio.

"So when was the piazza built?"

"*Built* is not the right word," his uncle began, folding up his paper. "It gives the idea of something born at a particular moment in time, according to a specific design. In fact, lots of artists from different periods worked on this place. During the Roman Age, it was occupied by the theatre and baths, and the city walls ran along one side of it. The buildings were abandoned when the barbarians arrived, and the inhabitants fled to the hills of Fiesole where they could better defend themselves. The theatre was transformed into a small, crenellated blockhouse, and what remained of the *insulae*—or 'condominiums'—was converted into makeshift barricades. Then, little by little, they started rebuilding among the ruins. By the year 1000 this entire area was filled with tower-houses."

"Blockhouses, city walls, fortifications... All they ever thought about was saving their skin!"

HISTORY & ARCHITECTURE

In Canto X of the Inferno, Dante meets Farinata degli Uberti. The proud Ghibelline, "lifting up his breast and brow as if he had great scorn of Hell," addresses the poet with the famous words: "O Tuscan, who makest thy way alive through the city of fire..." In the unforgettable lines that follow there are many references to bloody encounters between Guelphs and Ghibellines, such as the Battle of Montaperti (1260), which "stained the (river) Arbia red" (red with blood, of course). Despite their political differences, Dante shows great respect for Farinata, the man who urged that Florence be spared, when his allies wanted to raze the city to the ground.

COAT OF ARMS OF
THE TRIBUNAL

"Defence was doubtless their primary concern. Anyway, almost all of the towers in the area belonged to the same, powerful family: the Uberti. One of them was named Farinata, and he was the head of the Ghibellines. Do you remember who they were?"

"The emperor's supporters. They had it in for the pope-loving Guelphs."

"Very good. Near the end of the 1200s, the Guelphs defeated Farinata in a terrible battle outside of Florence. His family and their supporters were exiled, and their tower-houses were levelled. Moreover, the area where the Uberti houses once stood was said to be cursed, so that no one could ever build another house on it. That's how the piazza was born."

"Cursed, huh? They couldn't just let bygones be bygones."

"In 1298 the city rulers—the so-called *priori*—decided to build a large new building where they could hold their meetings. They called in the usual Arnolfo, who had already built up half the city. To save on building costs, Arnolfo incorporated existing towers (in this case, the towers of the exiled Foraboschi family) into the new structure. As they did with the Bargello, the new bell tower was erected on top of the tallest tower, known as *della Vacca*—the Cow's Tower. The tower you see is one hundred metres tall. The building would come to be known as the Palazzo della Signoria only later, and was smaller than it is today.

The oldest section is the large cube rising above the other sections: bulky and crenellated, a genuine castle. The problem was that as soon as the building was finished, they realized that the square was too small for it. So the government started buying the neighbouring houses in order to tear them down and make room. It took almost a hundred years, but in the end the piazza assumed its current proportions, and was paved over with bricks laid in a herring-bone pattern. After a while, it became clear that the iron-rimmed

68

MERCHANTS (CALIMALA)	MONEYCHANGERS' GUILD	WOOL GUILD	SILK GUILD	PHYSICIANS AND APOTHECARIES	FURRIERS' GUILD	BUTCHERS' GUILD

carriage wheels were ruining the pavement, so people were forbidden to cross it except on foot: thus was born the first pedestrian zone in the history of Florence. They built the Trade Tribunal along the short side of the piazza—it's the building with the emblems of the guilds decorating the façade. Specially appointed judges would keep an eye on commerce and resolve disputes between merchants, both foreign and Florentine."

"Slow down, I can't keep up with you! Finish telling me about Palazzo Vecchio."

"By the end of the 1400s, the original medieval edifice was no longer large enough to hold public gatherings, so they decided to add a new wing especially for the representatives of the *popolo*. If you look at the building from the Tribunal, it's easy to tell which section was added on: it has a sloping roof and larger windows. Another hundred years later, the last section was added. It extends along the downhill road, beyond the new hall. Of course, that meant a new home had to be found for the lion mascots that the Florentines kept in cages behind the palace. They didn't call that street Via dei Leoni for nothing."

LOGGIA DEI LANZI & STATUES

"And the loggia?"

"It serves as an open-air museum today, but it was built for a practical purpose. It's a funny story, really. The priors only held office for two months. With every changing of the guard, they would have a ceremony in front of the palace doors complete with banners, trumpets and Very Important Guests. The archbishop of Ravenna was invited to one of these ceremonies, and he showed up dressed up to the nines, of course, in full regalia. Unfortunately for everyone involved, it started pouring rain, and the archbishop was drenched… and furious. Eager to avoid similar embarrassments, the Florentines decided to build a large loggia for their ceremonies. They called it the Loggia dei Priori when it was built, but it's better known today as the Loggia dei Lanzi."

"Why Lanzi?"

"It stands for *Lanzichenecchi*, or Landsknechts—the German soldiers who used to guard the palace."

"*German*…? Wait, what year are we talking about exactly?"

"These soldiers served as the Medici's private army, like the Swiss Guard do at the Vatican. Then, after a while, when the grand dukes felt more secure,

they were sent elsewhere, and the loggia filled up with statues. But the square had started filling up, too…"

"That fellow on the horse over there, and the fountain?"

"Yes. The equestrian monument was sculpted by Giambologna: it's a portrait of Cosimo I mounted in the style of a Roman emperor. His son Ferdinando commissioned it to honour his father, the first grand duke and the conqueror of Siena. That's the *Neptune Fountain* next to it: the Florentines call it *Biancone*, or 'Big Whitey,' because it's large but a bit ungainly. To think that in those days, when a girl reached marrying age, her mother would bring her here to show her what a man was like without any clothes on… Ammannati, the fountain's sculptor, showed Cosimo 'disguised' as the sea god Neptune—he's surrounded by marine creatures in bronze: nymphs, dancing Tritons…"

COSIMO I DE' MEDICI

"I rather like this idea of having your portrait done in costume: Roman emperors, sea gods…"

"The choice of costume was never taken lightly, as each character had a special symbolic value. If you portrayed a prince as the god of the sea, for example, you meant to celebrate his maritime ambitions. Now, if you were having your portrait done for this piazza, what character would *you* choose?"

"Mmm, let's see… I guess Batman astride his bat-horse would be cool."

Absorbed in their amiable discussion, the two left their table and

headed towards Palazzo Vecchio. A copy of Donatello's sculpture of *Judith slaying Holofernes* was waiting for them at the entrance.

"The original is inside," Uncle Charlie explained, "but it used to decorate the gardens of Palazzo Medici. It was moved here when the family was exiled. Here's another copy of Michelangelo's *David*, and this is Baccio Bandinelli's try at *Hercules and Cacus*." Charles pointed to the large sculptures on either side of the building's entrance.

"And who would this guy Cacus be?"

"A fire-breathing giant and the son of Vulcan. He lived on the Aventine Hill, in Rome, and one time when Hercules was in the neighbourhood, Cacus made the mistake of stealing four cows and four bulls from him. Hercules tore the roof off his cave and throttled him to death in his grip of steel. Then he rounded up the animals and went on his way."

"What about the statues under the loggia?"

THE CASTING OF "PERSEUS"

"*Perseus*, the most famous of all, has just got out of the restoration laboratory right under the Uffizi portico—he needed some attention after all those years out in the open. It's an amazing statue that shows Perseus holding up Medusa's head. She was the monster with snakes instead of hair…"

"And people would turn to stone just by looking at her—I know, I know. What I want to know is what did Perseus think he was doing? What was he planning to do with her head? Use it as a paperweight?"

"He had promised it to a king, you know. Medusa was a terrifying creature, and her two sisters were pretty hideous themselves. The Greeks called them the Gorgons, and claimed that they lived beyond the Ocean, in the Kingdom of Night. Perseus had quite a job on his hands. Fortunately, he got a little help from some nymphs: they lent him winged sandals, a cape that

made him invisible, and a sack to put Medusa's head in. But no one knew where to find her, except two old hags that stood guard at the edge of the shadows. They only had one eye between the two of them, and they took turns with it. Perseus managed to grab the eye while they were passing it, and forced them to talk. That's how he found Medusa."

"And then?"

"According to some, he grabbed her by the throat with his eyes closed. Others claim he watched her in the reflection of a polished shield that Athena held up for him like a mirror. At any rate, he chopped off Medusa's head, stuck it in the sack and flew away with his magic sandals, her sisters in furious pursuit. Or maybe he rode away on the winged horse Pegasus, who had just emerged from the monster's throat."

"So what did he do with the head?"

"He used it as a weapon on various occasions, and who can blame him? It petrified people in the truest sense of the word. It came pretty close to petrifying its sculptor—Benvenuto Cellini. He was friends with the Grand Duke, and they passed many an evening together restoring Etruscan figurines that the peasants kept finding outside Fiesole. At a certain point, Cellini became so obsessed with the *Perseus* that it nearly killed him."

"Gosh! What happened?"

"The statue is in bronze, and the casting technique chosen by Cellini was very long and complicated. In order to create a hollow sculpture like the ancient Greeks used to make, you first had to model the figure in clay and bake it. Then you coated it with a layer of wax, and very carefully modelled out the details. The whole thing was then covered with another layer of clay. The three layers were nailed together and baked in a furnace. The wax would melt and drip out through specially designed vents, and molten bronze was poured into the hollow left by the wax. The outer clay casing was then broken off, the nails and tubes removed, and the terracotta 'soul' pulled out through the base.

With the final touch-ups and everything, the process could take years. Now, when the statue is large and detailed, things get even trickier, as the molten metal doesn't distribute properly into all parts of the mould. The Grand Duke himself said Cellini was crazy to try it: *Benvenuto*, he warned, *this figure cannot succeed in bronze—the laws of art do not admit it.* In fact, the artist ran into all sorts of troubles, as he describes first-hand in his memoirs. *The labour*, he recalls, *was more than I could stand; yet I forced myself to strain every nerve and muscle.*"

"Well?"

"Picture this. It was raining cats and dogs. Wind and water were streaming in from the courtyard and cooling off the furnace. Nevertheless, things got so hot in there that at a certain point the roof caught fire, and it looked like it was going to cave in altogether. Cellini was reeling with exhaustion, and had a fever to boot. He was forced to leave the job right at the most critical moment, during the pouring of the bronze. *I feel more ill than I ever did in all my life*, he writes, *and verily believe that it will kill me before a few hours are over.* He told his assistants how to proceed with the casting, and *with despair at heart* went off to bed. He really *was* sick: he kept calling out *I am dying*, and honestly didn't think he'd live to see the morning. At a certain point… Wait, I want to read this to you. You'll love it: *While I was thus terribly afflicted, I beheld the figure of a man enter my chamber, twisted in his body into the form of a capital S. He raised a lamentable, doleful voice, like one who announces their last hour to men condemned to die upon the scaffold, and spoke these words: 'O Benvenuto! your statue is spoiled, and there is no hope whatever of saving it'.*"

"Yikes! What had gone wrong?"

"The furnace had gone out. Cellini let out a scream. He jumped out of bed like a banshee and ran back to work, howling insults and slapping his people around."

"And then?"

"He sent people up on the roof to extinguish the fire, which was raging more out of control than ever. The door was barricaded with tables, rugs and rags in an attempt to shelter the furnace from the rain. The furnace, in turn, exploded."

"Mission: Impossible!"

"There's more. The bronze wasn't fluid enough because with all that fire, the alloy had been consumed. Now, Cellini's dishes were made out of pewter, so he grabbed all he could find and threw them into the furnace. The metal regained a liquid consistency, and the casting of *Perseus* was brought to a glorious close."

"Wow!"

"Listen to this: *seeing my work finished, I fell upon my knees, and with all my heart gave thanks to God. After all was over, I turned to a plate of salad on a bench there, and ate with hearty appetite, and drank together with the whole crew. Afterwards I retired to bed, healthy and happy, for it was now two hours before morning, and slept as sweetly as though I had never felt a touch of illness.* He had never felt better. When the statue was finished, people still didn't believe it was possible, and they thought Benvenuto must be some kind of devil!"

The Hall of the Five Hundred

"Strange," Philip remarked. "I was expecting the typical gloomy courtyard of a medieval castle, but the walls and columns are all decorated here… Plus, I knew that most castles had a well to supply water in case of siege, but this one even has a fountain. What sort of a castle *is* this, anyway?"

"Before the 1500s, the courtyard looked pretty much the way you imagined it. It was completely redone for a royal wedding. Like I told you, the building used to be much smaller. For security reasons— and also to minimize the risk of corruption—the priors lived here for the entire length of their term, removed from their families and served by an all-male staff. But there were relatively few priors, and they didn't really need much space. It was Girolamo Savonarola who came up

VERROCCHIO'S "PUTTO WITH THE DOLPHIN" (THE ORIGINAL!) IN PALAZZO VECCHIO'S COURTYARD

with the idea to build a huge meeting hall here. Savonarola was the Dominican friar who ruled the city after Lorenzo the Magnificent died, right up until…"

"…they burned him at the stake in Piazza della Signoria. I read about that."

"Savonarola established a council of five hundred wise men to rule alongside the republican government. He thought it would make it easier to resist the Medici family, who were doing everything they could to get back in power. He ordered that the building be expanded to accommodate his new council, and that's how the Hall of the Five Hundred was born. It's on the first floor, right at the top of this double staircase. Come on, we're almost there."

"It's enormous!" Philip admired as they entered the hall.

"As usual, most of what you're looking at wasn't part of the original design. When it was first built, the room was simple and undecorated, with a trussed roof and bare walls. Speaking of which, the walls were supposed to be frescoed by Michelangelo and Leonardo da Vinci, but for various reasons nothing ever came of it. If you look at the roof, you'll notice that the room isn't perfectly rectangular. The short sides aren't parallel because they're the extension of the external walls of the building, which was shaped as a trapezoid. When Cosimo de' Medici became duke, he moved here into the old city hall."

THE RHINOCEROS WAS THE EMBLEM OF DUKE ALESSANDRO
(SEE PAGE 117)

GIORGIO VASARI, "MASSIMILIANO RAISING THE SIEGE OF LIVORNO" (DETAIL: THE WHOLE PAINTING IS MUCH, MUCH BIGGER!)

"Just in case they hadn't worked out who was boss."

"The Hall was converted into the throne room. Giorgio Vasari, Cosimo's trusted artist, frescoed it with scenes from victorious battles against Pisa and Siena. On the ceiling, he painted stories—some true, some invented—honouring his powerful patron. Cosimo chose his coronation as the backdrop for the central portrait: seen from a distance, he looks like God surrounded by angels..."

FRANCESCO'S STUDIOLO & ELEONORA'S APARTMENTS

"Back to their camouflaging tricks again! What is this room, anyway? So tiny and packed with paintings..."

"This is what's known as the *Studiolo*, or 'little study', of Cosimo's son, Francesco: you remember him from the Duomo façade, Cellini's buddy. He was very much the solitary type, and spent entire days cooped up in here, leafing through his beloved books on alchemy. And watch out: the paintings conceal cabinets where he kept his collections."

"What did he collect?"

BARTOLOMEO AMMANNATI, "THE GODDESS OPI"
(STUDIOLO OF FRANCESCO)

AGNOLO BRONZINO, "ELEONORA DE TOLEDO WITH HER SON GIOVANNI" (UFFIZI)

"Vases, coins, all sorts of curiosities —some of them are still displayed at Palazzo Pitti."

"Are those his parents in the oval frame?"

"Yes. His mother was a Spanish lady named Eleonora, who was both beautiful and rich. She was just sixteen when she married Cosimo. You can imagine what a nightmare it must have been, trying to house an entire royal court in a medieval palace lacking all conveniences... There weren't even any fireplaces, as the priors had lived a Spartan life."

"Furnishing a castle... I wouldn't even know where to begin. Oh well, I don't suppose I'll run into *that* problem any time soon."

"They started adding on lots of new rooms, and even entire apartments. In one of the additions, each room is dedicated to a mythological character: Hercules, Jupiter... and on the terrace, the terrible Saturn who ate his own children."

A steep stairway led Charles and Philip up to the vertiginous gallery that crosses the Hall of the Five Hundred. From there, they entered Eleonora's Apartments.

"These are the rooms that the young duchess chose as her own—coincidentally, the same ones that the priors had lived in before her. The rooms have a Renaissance look as Vasari took it upon himself to modernize the stairways, ceilings and

FRANCESCO HAD AS HIS PERSONAL EMBLEM A WEASEL HOLDING IN ITS TEETH A SPRIG OF RUE, AN EVERGREEN SHRUB WITH STRONG-SCENTED LEAVES: IT WAS THOUGHT THAT WEASELS CARRIED RUE IN THEIR MOUTHS TO KEEP AWAY POISONOUS TOADS, WHO WERE REPELLED BY ITS POWERFUL ODOUR. ABOVE THE WEASEL IS THE MOTTO "AMAT VICTORIA CURAM" ('VICTORY LOVES PRUDENCE').

GIOVANNI STRADANO, "THE ALCHEMIST'S LABORATORY" (STUDIOLO OF FRANCESCO)

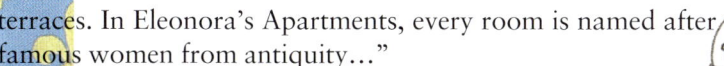

terraces. In Eleonora's Apartments, every room is named after famous women from antiquity..."

"Let's see... *Sala Verde*. The Green Room?"

"...except for the first, smarty-pants, which is obviously named after the colour of its walls."

They crossed the Room of the Sabine Women—once reserved for the royal ladies-in-waiting—and proceeded into the Room of Esther.

"This was the priors' dining room. They washed their hands in the large basin in the centre of the wall. The water that flowed from the faucet was merely rainwater, channelled down the rain gutters into in a holding tank behind the wall. This corner room, on the other hand, is dedicated to Penelope."

"Ulysses' wife, the one who spent her days sewing... or was it weaving?"

"Bravo. As you can see, this is a well-lit room, and the duchess used it for so-called women's work."

"Uncle... I'm beginning to feel a little tired."

"We'll go in a minute. But first I wanted to show you a very special room."

Uncle Charlie led his nephew across the *Udienze*, or Audience Room, into the Map Room.

"Boy, that globe is huge! Too bad it won't fit on my desk."

"It's a genuine antique. Try to find Australia, for example."

"It's not even on here... In compensation, it's got some great-looking cannibals!"

"Classic. Take a look at the maps, too: unexplored or unfamiliar territory was always full of monsters and strange beasts."

"Are there cabinets behind these panels, too?"

"Naturally. One of the maps even hides a secret passageway that leads to the outside."

"*Indiana Jones and the Palazzo of Doom*. All that's missing are trapdoors lined with razor-sharp blades!"

As he was leaving, Philip noticed a curious little figure: a turtle... with a sail. It was carved on one of the wooden panels of the doorway leading into the Sala dei Duecento.

"That's one of Cosimo's trademarks," Charles explained. "As usual, he was inspired by his favourite Roman emperor. The Latin motto above the turtle reads *Festina lente*, which means 'hurry up slowly'."

"My very sentiments—let's hurry up slowly to a good restaurant!"

79

THE PORCELLINO

"You ate like a little pig, as usual," Uncle Charlie teased, "so now I'm taking you to see a kindred soul."

Philip attributed his uncle's cryptic remark to the small flask of red wine that the archaeologist had polished off with lunch: its pernicious effects were just now becoming apparent... After a few minutes, the two came to a fountain with a large bronze statue of a boar.

"Allow me to introduce the *Porcellino*, or Piglet."

"Piglet—you're kidding!"

"That's what they call it. It's a copy of a famous sculpture by Pietro Tacca, an artist from the 1600s. He, in turn, had copied it from an ancient Roman marble statue housed in the Uffizi Gallery. The Romans, on the other hand, had copied it from a Greek statue in bronze! According to tradition, everyone who rubs the *Porcellino*'s nose will return to Florence one day."

Philip promptly hopped in line.

"The loggia behind us is called *Mercato Nuovo*, the New Market. It's a just a street market today, but it used to be where silk merchants and goldsmiths came to do business. Their guild was based here in Via Por Santa Maria, this street here off to the right."

"I've been meaning to ask you... These guilds were called *arti*..."

"The word for 'art' in Italian also used to mean 'corporation'."

"So what are they making at that little stand over there?"

"We can come back some other time to enjoy one of life's greatest pleasures: a tripe *panino*!"

"Why put off until tomorrow what you can do today?"

"We finished lunch thirty seconds ago!" Uncle Charlie scolded his nephew, horrified. "My sister gave birth to an extraterrestrial life form! Wait—where's my copy of the standard SETI greeting? I always carry it on me just in case..."

Philip, in the meantime, was watching the various phases of *lampredotto* preparation, hypnotized.

ORSANMICHELE

The two strolled down Via Calzaioli and turned onto Via dell'Arte della Lana.

"This, my boy, is the church of Orsanmichele. The name is short for *Orto di San Michele*, which means 'St Michael's Orchard'."

"It's funny. You wouldn't even guess it was a church if it weren't for all these saints' statues. Three stories high, and it doesn't even have a bell tower!"

"And look at the walls: they're heavy and rough towards the top but slender at the ground floor—at some points they're fretworked like lace. The floor isn't tiled in marble or other valuable materials, but paved in stone, like that of a market square. It *is* a weird building, indeed, but there's a good explanation. Before the arcades were walled up, this was an open portico: the loggia of the old grain market. The land where the monks of St Michael used to tend their orchard was turned into a grain market. Arnolfo di Cambio—the architect of the Duomo and Palazzo Vecchio— built a brick-and-wooden awning to protect the stands. But one day the loggia was burnt down in a fire. According to legend, the only column left standing was the one painted with an image of the Virgin Mary. News of the miracle spread fast, and people would stop here at sunset to pray."

"Why wait until sunset?"

"Because it was still used as a market during the day. In 1337, the city had a new 'fireproof' loggia built with stone piers and brick vaulting like we saw at the New Market. Since they needed a dry, ventilated place to store grain for times of famine, they added on two large rooms above the loggia. Having the market below and the granary above was very convenient—not to mention that an elevated warehouse in the heart of the city would be safer from mice, thieves and floods. A stairway was carved out

of the pier to the left of the entrance: it was used by city workers to access the grain deposit. There's a rectangular trapdoor in the vaulting that they leaned out of to see who was knocking at the door. They used a cord-and-pulley system to hoist the sacks of grain up through the windows on the upper floor."

"And to get them back down again?"

"There were specially designed chutes: the grain would slide right down, nice and easy. Those two piers on the left are hollow, and you can still see the slots that the grain passed through."

"Ingenious."

"And there's more. Florence had never been as rich as it was during the 1300s: the main streets were all paved, you know, and costly stone buildings had replaced the makeshift, wartime ones. Then the fateful year of 1348 came along, and with it, the plague. The desperate Florentines got together in the market and begged the Virgin to bring the epidemic to an end, which she promptly did. In gratitude, they commissioned a large altarpiece in her honour. It shows the *Madonna and Child Enthroned*, and was painted by one of Giotto's pupils, Bernardo Daddi."

"I suppose it's still around here somewhere."

"It sure is, right inside, in that monumental tabernacle sculpted in white marble and inlaid with coloured glass paste. It was designed by sculptor and architect Andrea Orcagna. Meanwhile, an ever-growing number of faithful, sick and needy, were coming here to pray. To accommodate them, the loggia was transformed into an oratory. The arcades were closed off and the market was moved elsewhere. It didn't take long for the place to fill up with *ex voto*—offerings that reproduce the entire figure, or even individual body parts—of the people healed by the Virgin Mary. They were hung everywhere, even from those rings up on the ceiling."

"But you still had to pass through the church to get to the granary above."

"In fact, it was bad form. That's why they made the catwalk that runs from the building

of the Wool Guild to the old granary. It's set up as a museum now. Before we leave, make sure you take a look at the oratory's stained-glass windows. They illustrate the miracles of the Madonna of Orsanmichele, and are among the oldest in Florence."

"And now for the sculpture in the tabernacles," Uncle Charlie continued, once they were outside. "The various civic corporations were all eager to sponsor such a popular oratory. The city cleverly decided to entrust its care and decoration... to all of them. The Major Guilds, which were the wealthiest, provided a statue of their patron saint for the niches on the façade. The Minor Guilds commissioned frescoes or images in glazed terracotta."

"Who's that saint with the shield and armour?"

"St George. Donatello sculpted him for the Swordmakers and Armourers' Guild. He was still very young and not yet well-known when he did it, so they gave him a shallow niche, on the corner pier that the stairway runs through. At any rate, this, too..."

"Is a copy. And we'll see the original..."

"At the Bargello. All in good time."

SANTA CROCE

THE PIAZZA & HISTORIC FOOTBALL

S anta Croce?"

Philip and Uncle Charlie had entered the piazza after a scenic walk through the medieval streets of Florence.

"You guessed it. Ever since the 1300s, this square has been the site of tournaments, parties and jousts. When the need arose—brace yourself—it was even transformed into a football field. This is where the famous football matches in costume were held—and still are to this day."

"Never heard of them. In *costume*?"

"Tennis shoes aside, the players' outfits look like they're straight out of the 16th century."

"But what are the rules like? And who invented it?"

THE PIAZZA & HISTORIC FOOTBALL

"A similar game probably existed as far back as Greek and Roman times. It's always been very popular here in Florence. The game is fairly violent and requires a lot of strength and skill. Still, it was never hard to convince young men from good families to play: they knew that plenty of girls would be in the audience, and it gave them a chance to strut their stuff—you know how it is. It was also a perfect opportunity to settle old scores without risking a night in the cooler: it was just a game, but the blows they landed were real enough."

"And the teams?"

"There were four of them, one for each of the city quarters: the Whites of Santo Spirito, the Greens of San Giovanni, the Reds of Santa Maria Novella, and the Blues of Santa Croce. The most memorable game of all time was played on 17 February 1530. The imperial troops of Charles V were camped right outside the city walls, but the game proceeded as planned. The Florentines wanted to show that they couldn't care less about the emperor's siege: to prove their point, they even sent buglers up on the roof of Santa Croce."

"Overkill! That must have been dangerous, though."

"Very much so. In fact, a cannonball whizzed by their heads at a certain point, but no one was hurt and the game went on as if nothing had happened. They stopped holding the matches during the 1700s, but the tradition was revived in 1930 and has been a regular event ever since. They play every 24 June, for the feast of St John the Baptist."

"You still haven't explained the rules to me."

85

GIORGIO VASARI & GIOVANNI STRADANO, "THE SIEGE OF FLORENCE" (PALAZZO VECCHIO, ROOM OF CLEMENT VII

"The game lasts an hour. There are two teams with twenty-seven players each. The rectangular field is covered with sand, and divided down the middle by a white line. Nets are hung at the short ends of the field, and the idea is to get the ball into the adversaries' net, scoring the so-called *caccia* or goal. Each goal is accompanied by a shot from the culverins, which are antique cannons with a long, slender barrel."

"It sounds a little like rugby."

"Yes, a combination of rugby, soccer and street-fighting. A pretty strong cocktail, what with all the shoving, kicking and slapping around… an hour-long brawl. Oh yes, and the winners get a calf."

"I want to go!"

"We'll see. We definitely don't want to miss the pre-game procession. It's spectacular: more than five hundred people in costume and armour who parade through the centre with drums and trumpets… Anyway, the piazza was more peaceful during the 1200s, when the Franciscans lived there."

"Followers of St Francis of Assisi—the saint who talked to animals."

"And who sacrificed his riches to lead a life of poverty. A lot of

GIOVANNI STRADANO, "KNIGHTS JOUSTING IN SANTA CRO
(PALAZZO VECCHIO, APARTMENTS OF ELEONO

people—well, *some* people—followed his example, and churches and convents were built to accommodate them. In Florence, the Franciscans settled here, in what was at the time a little church outside the city walls, in a marshy area home to the most humble wool-workers. Their sermons soon attracted large crowds, and were held in this piazza. Then, at the end of the 1200s, they started building the Gothic church you see in front of you."

THE CHURCH OF SANTA CROCE

"The façade doesn't look particularly Gothic to me… and it doesn't have much to do with Franciscan simplicity either. This isn't another one of those…"

"Later additions! Exactly. In fact, the façade was put up during the 1800s."

"What can I say? I can spot certain things a mile off."

"You see that plaque on the façade? It marks the level that the water reached during the flood of 1966."

"That high! It must have caused some awful damage."

"That's putting it mildly. You'll get a taste of it when we go into the museum next to the church. Let's go inside."

Upon entering, Philip was immediately struck by the large number of altars that lined the church walls.

"Practically all of the altars and monuments were put in after the 1500s. Many of them hold the remains of famous Italians like Michelangelo and Galileo, but some of them are empty. The church was designed by Arnolfo di Cambio…"

"Not him again!"

"…in that soaring Gothic style we've come to recognize, with its lovely stained-glass windows. The church's wooden roof, however, interrupts the soaring line of the lancet arches."

"A less-Gothic sort of Gothic."

"Exactly. The walls were originally frescoed with stories of the saints. The Franciscans talked about them during their sermons and even re-enacted them in *sacre rappresentazioni*, a sort of religious theatre with the piazza here serving as the stage. Many of the old frescoes were lost, but there are still some at the back of the church, behind the main altar and in the chapels. The chapel frescoes were commissioned by wealthy Florentine families of the 1300s, who as usual tried to outdo one another in depicting their favourite saints."

INSIDE SANTA CROCE THERE ARE FUNERARY MONUMENTS TO MANY FAMOUS ITALIANS: MICHELANGELO (SCULPTOR, PAINTER AND ARCHITECT), VITTORIO ALFIERI (POET), NICCOLÒ MACHIAVELLI (HISTORIAN AND THINKER), LEONARDO BRUNI (SCHOLAR AND POLITICIAN), GIOACCHINO ROSSINI (COMPOSER), LEON BATTISTA ALBERTI (ARCHITECT AND PHILOSOPHER), GALILEO (SCIENTIST, SEE CHAPTER 12). THE TOMBS OF THESE FAMOUS MEN INSPIRED UGO FOSCOLO'S WELL-KNOWN POEM "ON THE SEPULCHRES" (1807).

GIOTTO & CIMABUE

"It wouldn't be complete without St Francis, of course," Uncle Charlie continued, entering the Bardi Chapel. "These frescoes illustrate scenes from his life. Giotto painted them. If you compare them with the baptistery mosaics, you see at once that Giotto has a new take on the body, space and stories. Look at the St Francis on that gilded panel painting: it's a skinny little figure, out of proportion. Giotto's friars, on the other hand, are very 'physical' and well-fed. In the panel, the birds are stylized, and the figures are lined up Indian-file; Giotto tried to make his backgrounds—and particularly the position of his figures in space—as natural and realistic as possible. The most remarkable fresco in the cycle is the *Renunciation of Worldly Goods*. In this scene, Francis strips himself of his elegant clothes and hands them over to his father. He stands there naked in the middle of the town square of

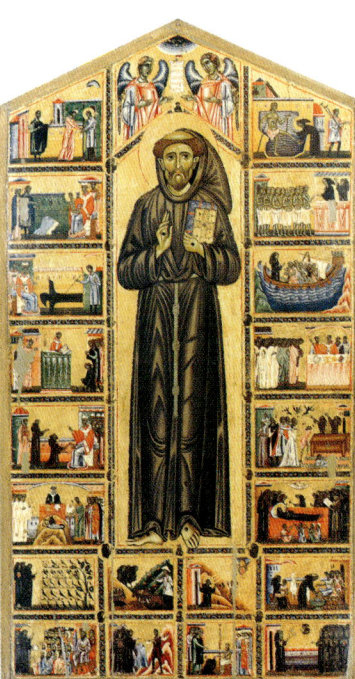

Assisi, obviously creating something of a scandal among the onlookers. Giotto is wonderfully effective in portraying the characters' emotions: Francis' father, for example—the one in the yellow tunic—is beside himself with rage, and they barely manage to keep him from beating his son in public. Then there are the women carrying the children away: such a showy and revolutionary gesture was hardly appropriate for innocent eyes. And finally, there's the bishop who covers Francis with his own cloak: the rebel is welcomed into the bosom of the Church."

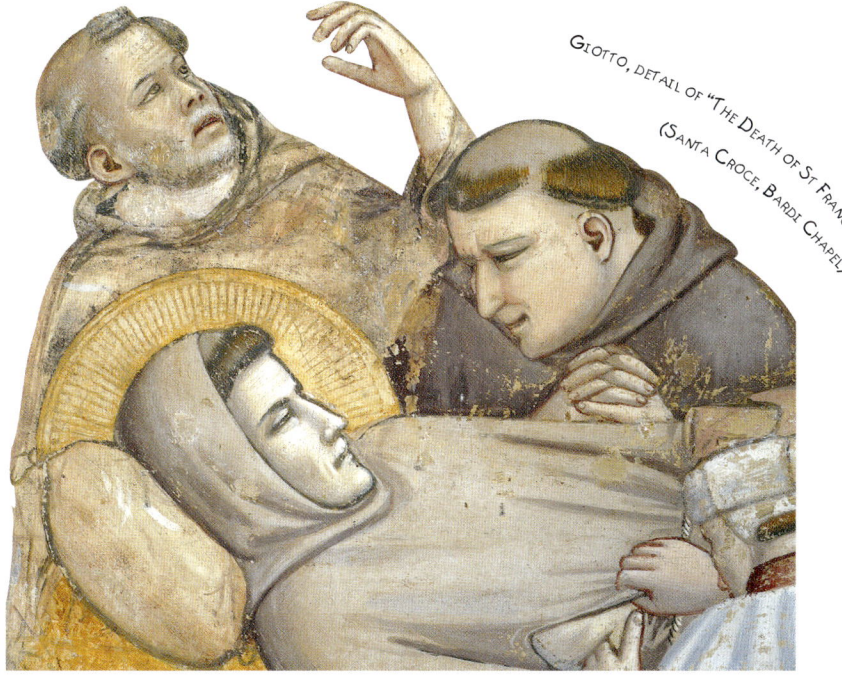

GIOTTO, DETAIL OF "THE DEATH OF ST FRANCIS" (SANTA CROCE, BARDI CHAPEL)

"Clear as clear can be."

"It had to be—or illiterate people wouldn't be able to understand the story. This way, even the poor and uneducated could 'read' the images. Come, there's a miracle in the other chapel."

The two moved on to the Bardi di Vernio Chapel. "These frescoes illustrate the miracles of St Sylvester. One of them is kind of funny. The artist is Maso di Banco, who was one of Giotto's followers. Pretend you're a commoner from the Dark Ages and try to read the dragon scene."

"Let's see. The guy with the halo must be the saint. He's shown twice, which means that the story is told in two parts."

"Very good."

"The saint is in the middle… and he tells those two on the ground to get back on their feet…"

"And he calls a foul for simulation! Come on, we're not talking soccer here!"

"Wait a minute. They were on the ground, and now they're standing. I get it: he brought them back to life!"

"That's more like it. Now, the ruins: they're overgrown with grass, which means they must be very ancient. Then there's the marble column that divides the scene in two…"

"Ancient Rome?"

"Bravo! The scene unfolds in the crumbling forum. The two resuscitated characters are sorcerers. But what do you think happened to them?"

"Let's see… There's a dragon on the left, and St Sylvester is holding its mouth

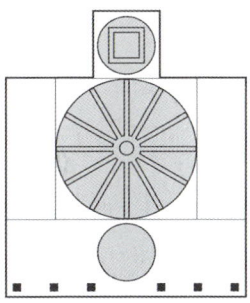

shut. The other character is plugging its nose... The wizards were felled by the dragon's stinky breath!"

"Congratulations. You have a brilliant career as a medieval commoner ahead of you... or as an art historian, maybe?"

"Thanks to this Maso guy: he painted what it took to tell the story. Nothing more, nothing less."

Later, in the Santa Croce museum, Philip got a first-hand look at one of the many victims of the 1966 flood: Cimabue's *Crucifix*. Cimabue was Giotto's teacher, and his work marked the passage from medieval art to the new realism of Giotto's work.

"It's in terrible shape! The face and body are practically wiped out altogether. But wasn't it hanging in the church, above the main altar?"

"If it only had been, it wouldn't have been ruined. Unfortunately, it was right where you see it now. It was washed over in mud along with the other pieces here in the museum."

IN THE MIDDLE AGES CHURCHES WERE USUALLY PLANNED AS A LATIN CROSS, WITH ONE LONG ARM (THE NAVE AND APSE) AND ONE SHORT ARM (THE TRANSEPT). THEN CAME THE RENAISSANCE, WITH ITS PASSION FOR ORDERED, 'RATIONAL' SPACE; ARCHITECTS BECAME FASCINATED BY THE CIRCLE, THE MOST PERFECT OF ALL SHAPES, AND BEGAN TO DESIGN 'CENTRALLY PLANNED' BUILDINGS, THAT IS TO SAY ONES WHICH WERE LAID OUT SYMMETRICALLY AROUND A CENTRAL POINT: THEY WERE EITHER CIRCULAR, OR SQUARE, OR IN THE SHAPE OF A GREEK CROSS (A CROSS WITH ARMS OF EQUAL LENGTH). BRUNELLESCHI LOVED PLAYING AROUND WITH GEOMETRICAL SHAPES (SEE THE OLD SACRISTY IN SAN LORENZO), AND HE TOO WAS SOON ATTRACTED TO THE CENTRALISED PLAN. THE PAZZI CHAPEL (BUILT FOR THE FAMILY WHO WOULD LATER LEAD THE UNSUCCESSFUL CONSPIRACY AGAINST LORENZO THE MAGNIFICENT) WAS HIS FIRST ATTEMPT. THE PLAN IS MORE OF LESS CENTRALISED: IN THE MIDDLE IS A RECTANGLE WIDER THAN IT IS LONG, WITH A PORTICO IN FRONT AND A SQUARE APSE BEHIND, CONTAINING THE ALTAR. ALL THREE SPACES ARE SURMOUNTED BY A DOME: THE LARGEST ONE IS IN THE CENTRE, WITH A CONICAL ROOF AND A LANTERN, AND THE TWO SMALLER ONES ARE IN FRONT AND BEHIND. WHEN BRUNELLESCHI DIED, THE WORK WAS STILL UNFINISHED, AND IT IS STILL DEBATED WHETHER THE FINAL RESULT REFLECTED HIS ORIGINAL PLANS. FILIPPO WAS NOT EASILY SATISFIED. SHORTLY AFTER DESIGNING THE PAZZI CHAPEL HE PLANNED, FOR THE CAMALDOLESE MONKS, SANTA MARIA DEGLI ANGELI, THE FIRST CENTRALLY PLANNED CHURCH OF THE RENAISSANCE, WHICH UNFORTUNATELY WAS NEVER COMPLETED: A CENTRAL OCTAGON SURMOUNTED BY A DOME, WITH SIXTEEN EXTERNAL SIDES; INSIDE, ONE CHAPEL PER SIDE (THEREFORE EIGHT); OUTSIDE, A NICHE EVERY OTHER SIDE (THEREFORE EIGHT, AGAIN). STUFF THAT MAKES YOUR HEAD SPIN...

SANTA MARIA NOVELLA & SAN LORENZO

THE SUN, SYMBOL OF THE DOMINICAN ORDER

SANTA MARIA NOVELLA: THE SQUARE & CHURCH

ere's a trivia question for you: what movie won the most Academy Awards in the history of cinema?"

"*Titanic*. It got eleven of them."

"That's right, but I had another one in mind."

"Let's see… Oh yeah, that larger-than-life epic they're always replaying on TV: *Ben Hur*!"

"From 1959. And you remember that one incredible scene… Hold on a minute: who won ten awards?"

"Don't change the subject. You were talking about the chariot race scene."

"What I meant was, if you found yourself in this square at the end of the 1500s, you might have witnessed a similar scene."

Philip, Charles and Giulia were in Piazza Santa Maria Novella, once serving as the track for the *Palio dei Cocchi* chariot races organized by Cosimo I. The track ran around the two obelisks situated at the extremes of the square, and wooden bleachers were set up for the spectators. The grand duke and his court took their places under the portico, on a raised platform surrounded by standards.

THE SWELLING SAIL, A SIGN OF GOOD FORTUNE, THE EMBLEM OF GIOVANNI DI PAOLO RUCELLAI

"The square wasn't originally built as a racetrack. It was designed to hold the church's overflow of worshippers."

"Like at Santa Croce."

"Exactly. This convent, too, belonged to a mendicant order, the Dominicans. When they first arrived in Florence, they settled in a small church outside the city walls, just like the Franciscans, but on the other side of the city. Over time, they expanded it and decorated it with the help of two friar architects, Sisto and Ristoro. There's a cemetery to the right of the church: it's just a simple plot of land, in keeping with the tradition of these orders."

"Those walls that enclose it don't look all that simple."

"It's true," Giulia agreed. "Those niches along the wall hold sarcophagi made of expensive green and white marble. They belonged to wealthy Florentine families. Even today, the street that runs along the church is called the Via degli Avelli, which means 'Street of the Tombs'."

"They ran out of money at a certain point and had to interrupt construction", continued Charles. "150 years passed before Giovanni di Paolo Rucellai decided to do something about it. He had made his fortune marketing purple fabric—a shade that no one else knew how to make. Anyway, he called Leon Battista Alberti to finish the church, façade included."

"The façade reminds me a lot of San Minato," Philip observed. "Geometric figures, green and white marble…"

"That sort of temple surrounding the glass eye at the centre of the façade is an homage to classic architecture, which was very prized during the Renaissance. Alberti invented that type of scroll moulding that connects the upper with the lower part of the façade: they are called 'volutes,' and they quickly became very fashionable. Some time later, a fri-

ar interested in astronomy added two instruments that served to study the motion of the stars and planets: that sort of sundial, and the instrument on the left, known as an armillary sphere."

"The interior is decidedly Gothic," Philip announced, "and those multicoloured stained-glass windows let a beautiful light in... Listen Giulia, about this Renaissance thing—how were Renaissance people different from medieval ones?"

MASACCIO'S "TRINITY"

"Take a look at this fresco," she began. "It's the *Trinity* by Masaccio, one of the greatest painters of the 1400s. God the Father stands behind Christ the Son, and the Holy Spirit is represented by the white dove between the two. It's a truly emblematic painting, and it highlights some of the aspects of the Renaissance spirit. To begin with, take a look at Jesus' body. It's practically an anatomical study. God is no longer distant, unreachable in a golden sky or lost amongst the clouds: he's standing in a chapel that looks like Brunelleschi himself could have built it. The scene is painted from our point of view: we see the higher figures from the bottom up, and the lower ones from the top down."

"In perspective, you mean."

"There's the magic word. Here, for the first time in the history of painting, Masaccio painstakingly applied the rules of linear perspective. In painting the chapel, he used a virtually flawless system of perspective with a central vanishing point. Perspective not only helps to distribute the figures rationally on the fresco, but it also makes the viewer feel like he could almost enter into the scene. The painting effectively becomes a continuation of real space."

"Don't panic! We'll talk more about perspective later," Uncle Charlie whispered to Philip reassuringly.

"The couple kneeling on the steps are Mr and Mrs Lensi, who are

buried here. They're the same size as the Virgin Mary and St John—they're even dressed similarly. Only their position and the fact that they don't have haloes distinguish them from the two sacred figures. You remember the mosaics in the baptistery—that enormous Christ and the tiny humans? Masaccio doesn't go for it: he puts both the sacred characters and his contemporaries on the same level, in the same space, in a Renaissance chapel."

"I see. There are no longer differences in proportion, background or clothing. All of the characters are seen as they would be in a photograph, and not larger or smaller depending on their importance."

"Therein lies the secret: in the eye of the beholder. The supernatural is no longer seen dominating and oppressing mankind; now it is man himself who observes and puts into order the universe that surrounds him."

"A rational vision centred around man and inspired by ancient thought," Charles summed up. "A view Masaccio shared with Brunelleschi."

GHIRLANDAIO'S STORIES

The three made their way behind the marble tabernacle of the main altar. Below a splendid stained-glass window, a fresco cycle by Ghirlandaio was waiting for them. The frescoes told the *Stories of the Madonna and St John the Baptist.*

"You remember Palazzo Davanzati?" the archaeologist prompted. "Here—among other things—the painter depicts many of the objects, clothes and furniture that we saw at the museum."

"Domenico Ghirlandaio," Giulia continued, "garnished his sacred scenes with details from the daily life of his time. He even added relatives, friends, and colleagues of the Tornabuoni's, a rich Florentine family related to the Medici."

"There's a street named after them. We walked down it yesterday—the one lined with classy designer shops!"

"And speaking of luxury... here's the

A.D. MCC (1200)

DOMENICO GHIRLANDAIO, "APPROBATION OF THE RULE OF ST FRANCIS" (CHU OF SANTA TRINITA, SASSETTI CHAPEL

1400

Florentine *lettuccio* bed we were talking about, with its handy chests. And look at the room itself: it's covered with wooden carvings. Up at the top, there's a glazed terracotta frieze decorated with putti—you know, those lovely, puffy little kids… And there's another room painted on this wall. Those women bringing gifts to the new mothers are the Tornabuoni daughter and daughter-in-law. They both died very young, during childbirth: a common occurrence in those days. When you have time, make sure you stop by the church of Santa Trinita…"

"At the foot of Via Tornabuoni," Charles chimed in.

"The Sassetti Chapel there is decorated with another one of Ghirlandaio's frescoes. It was supposed to illustrate the life of St Francis, but he took the opportunity to portray Lorenzo the Magnificent with a whole flock of children and tutors. In the background you can make out monuments and details of Florence the way it was back then, including the Palazzo Vecchio, Loggia dei Lanzi and Santa Trinita bridge."

"Listen, uncle…"

"Let me guess: you're hungry."

"Well, now that you mention it…"

"Let's go to the San Lorenzo market," Giulia suggested. "It's not far, and there are many *trattorie* and stands where we can grab a snack."

"A snack?! You don't know Philip. He's capable of eating half the market."

"And that place you were telling me about yesterday, the one with all the street stands?"

"The *Mercato Centrale*, or Central Market, and the San Lorenzo market surrounding it. Forward, march! Afterwards, we'll take a look at the church—another one of Brunelleschi's masterpieces."

THE CHURCH OF SAN LORENZO

"Here it is: San Lorenzo, the Medici's parish. The Medici, as you know, were the Florentine family that dominated the city's political scene for more than three centuries, from the early 1400s through the early 1700s."

"What's wrong with the façade?"

"It just doesn't have the final marble facing. For the umpteenth time, they ran out of money before the façade was finished. It's a shame, really, because Michelangelo had done a few nice designs… The building that you're looking at was begun in the early 1400s. There was a much smaller church there previously, one of the oldest in Florence. Then Lorenzo's great-grandfather, Giovanni di Bicci, made his fortune as a banker. He decided to transform the little medieval church into a family temple, and asked Brunelleschi to give it an overhaul. As you can see, the white and grey interior is very subdued: there are none of the sublime soaring lines or heady heights that characterize Gothic architecture. The beauty here lies in the elegant, restrained simplicity with which the space is organized: a space where 'man is the measure.' Cosimo the Elder took over the project's financing where his father had left off: like him, he was an able businessman and politician, but of a different generation. Religious sentiments had changed, as had artistic tastes. Spaces had to be definite, comprehensible, as orderly as Masaccio's paintings: the triumph of perspective…"

"While we're on the subject, what exactly *is* perspective? I mean, give me the most accurate…"

"It's the technique that allows us to transfer reality as we see it onto a flat surface: from three dimensions into two. For example: let's say you turn your back

to the portal and look towards the main altar —the distant columns will seem smaller than the ones closer to you; the further away, the smaller they seem… Similarly, the lines of the floor tiles seem to get closer together as they recede. Our eyes create that effect: of course the columns are

all the same height and the lines are parallel. But if you wanted to sketch the interior of a church on a piece of paper or on a canvas, you would have to recreate the optical illusion by drawing columns of differing heights and converging lines. Perspective studies the laws that create these optical illusions, and it had its finest moment during the Renaissance."

"OK, I get it. Hey, Giulia, where's that Medici chapel you mentioned?"

THE CLOISTER OF SAN LORENZO, IMMEDIATELY TO THE LEFT OF THE CHURCH, WAS REBUILT AND ENLARGED BY MICHELOZZO. FROM HERE ONE CLIMBS THE STAIRS TO THE LAURENTIAN LIBRARY, WHICH HAS ONE OF THE MOST VALUABLE COLLECTIONS OF MANUSCRIPTS IN THE WORLD. THE COLLECTION HAS A TROUBLED HISTORY. IT WAS BEGUN BY COSIMO THE ELDER AND ENLARGED BY LORENZO THE MAGNIFICENT (THE MANUSCRIPT ON THE RIGHT HAS HIS PORTRAIT: AND HE CERTAINLY DESERVED IT, AS HE SPENT ENORMOUS SUMS OF MONEY SO THAT RARE MANUSCRIPTS COULD BE SOUGHT OUT AND COPIED), BUT IT WAS CONFISCATED IN 1494, WHEN THE MEDICI FAMILY WAS DRIVEN OUT OF FLORENCE. CARDINAL GIOVANNI DE' MEDICI (WHO LATER BECAME POPE AS LEO X) WAS COMPELLED TO BUY IT BACK; TO BE ON THE SAFE SIDE, HE TOOK IT WITH HIM TO ROME. IT WAS EVENTUALLY BROUGHT BACK TO FLORENCE BY HIS COUSIN GIULIO, POPE CLEMENT VII. AMONG ITS TREASURES—THE CODEX AMIATINUS OF THE BIBLE HAS BEEN CALLED "THE MOST BEAUTIFUL BOOK IN THE WORLD"— THERE ARE ANCIENT MANUSCRIPTS WHICH ARE INDISPENSABLE FOR RECONSTRUCTING WORKS BY FAMOUS GREEK AND LATIN WRITERS: THE TRAGIC POETS AESCHYLUS AND SOPHOCLES, VIRGIL (AUTHOR OF THE "AENEID") AND THE GREAT HISTORIAN TACITUS.

'HORSE'S-HEAD' MEDICI COAT OF ARMS WITH SEVEN B...

THE OLD SACRISTY

"Cosimo was never one to think small, and he wasn't about to settle for a simple private chapel. He hired Brunelleschi and Donatello to build and decorate a side room to the left of the main altar—the place is known as the Old Sacristy. It's completely geometrical: a cube with an umbrella-like, hemispherical dome. The whole thing is white, bordered with grey *pietra serena*. It's all very simple, really, very *measurable*. The space neither oppresses you nor makes you dizzy from

THE VESTIBULE OF THE LAURENTIAN LIBRARY (WITH ITS FAMOUS STAIRCASE) WAS DESIGNED BY MICHELANGELO

the height, but it develops around you in a rational way, making you feel at the centre of the universe. It was a completely new concept in those days, and people came especially to see it."

"And the tombs of Cosimo's parents?"

"They're under that marble table there. Not a very glamorous arrangement, perhaps, but practical: every day, before and after the service, the priests placed the chalice on the altar and knelt here in prayer. Thus, the memory of the dead was continually honoured. The sacristy also houses the tombs of Cosimo's children, Giovanni and Piero the Gouty."

"What about Cosimo himself?" Philip inquired once they were back in the nave.

"Right underneath us. He wanted to be buried under the pavement, in the centre of the church, right in front of the altar. Very much in keeping with his character: he had been at the centre of Florentine politics all his life, but always kept carefully out of the limelight."

"A sort of grey eminence…"

"A false modesty that served him well. And now, something completely different—the Medici Chapels!"

THE MEDICI CHAPELS

And something completely different they were indeed. Circling to the back of the church, the three arrived at the entrance of the Princes' Chapel.

"The Princes' Chapel and the New Sacristy are still part of the Laurentian complex, but they're a museum now."

Below the great dome of the chapel, Philip understood what Uncle Charlie was talking about. Neither the tomb-stones in Santa Reparata nor Cosimo's in San Lorenzo had prepared him for this. It was an extravagant, complex space, entirely covered with marbles of different colour and origin. The room

was so rich with hues and designs it was almost impossible to tell where the walls ended and the floor began.

"Nothing simple here..."

"The Roman emperors had a real passion for coloured marble, and Lorenzo the Magnificent and the grand dukes wanted nothing less. In the 1600s, Ferdinando I eventually decided to construct the large family mausoleum that his father Cosimo, the first grand duke, had only dreamed of. This is the result. The Medici—who were at that point absolute sovereigns—astonished not only foreign heads of state and diplomats, but their own subjects as well. You see, at the time, this was considered one of the wonders of the world! Those sixteen coats of arms in semi-precious stone represent the Tus-

TOMB OF GIULIANO, DUKE OF NEMOURS

"DAY"

102

can cities conquered and swiftly annexed into the grand duchy."

"I guess they were pretty well off…"

"That decoration with the diamond rings is one of the family emblems: it signified that the Medici, as well as being powerful, were as resistant and luminous as diamond."

"Modest, as usual."

"Modest? The original project was even more grandiose: the dome of the chapel was supposed to be covered with lapis lazuli and studded with gilded bronze stars! Unfortunately, the dynasty went extinct before the project was complete."

A short corridor led them into the New Sacristy.

"It reminds me of the one that Brunelleschi did," Philip observed, "even though this one's got more decorations and sculpture. It's just up near the top that the design gets simpler…"

"That's because it's supposed to represent the lifting of the soul from material to spiritual riches. Michelangelo was responsible for the design and statues. Above the tombs are portraits of Giuliano and Lorenzo…"

"The two brothers."

"No: *this* Giuliano was actually the *son* of Lorenzo the Magnificent, and was duke of Nemours; and *this* Lorenzo was his grandson, the duke of Urbino. Michelangelo portrayed them as Action and Thought personified. It seems that Giuliano's statue didn't really resemble him: someone pointed that out and…"

"But who cares now? After centuries, nobody's going to know the difference?"

"That's exactly what Michelangelo said! Look, the tomb of the brothers is there on the right, but it was never finished. The other statues, two men and two women, represent Dawn and Dusk, Day and Night."

They had seen about enough. Giulia suggested that they adjourn with a lovely sunset—you know where…

> **EPIGRAM BY GIOVANNI STROZZI ON THE "NIGHT" BY MICHELANGELO**
>
> "NIGHT, WHICH YOU SEE SO SWEETLY SLEEPING, WAS SCULPTED BY AN ANGEL IN THIS STONE, & BECAUSE SHE SLEEPS SHE LIVES: WAKE HER, IF YOU DON'T BELIEVE ME, & SHE'LL SPEAK TO YOU."
>
> **MICHELANGELO'S REPLY, PUT INTO THE MOUTH OF "NIGHT"**
>
> "GRATEFUL AM I FOR SLEEP, & FOR BEING OF STONE, WHILE ADVERSITY AND SHAME ENDURE; NOT TO SEE, NOT TO FEEL I DEEM GOOD FORTUNE; DO NOT WAKE ME, THEN—BY HEAVEN, SPEAK SOFTLY."

TOMB OF LORENZO, DUKE OF URBINO

"NIGHT"

PERSPECTIVE

WHAT DO YOU DO WHEN YOU WANT TO—OR HAVE TO—DRAW SOMETHING? LET ME GUESS: YOU GO INTO THE KITCHEN AND POUR OUT A GLASS OF YOUR FAVOURITE DRINK; YOU TURN ON THE STEREO, THE RADIO, THE TELEVISION — NOT ALL THREE AT ONCE, I HOPE—AND YOU SIT YOURSELF DOWN IN FRONT OF A BLANK SHEET OF PAPER, AN EMPTY CANVAS, OR A COMPUTER SCREEN; THEN YOU PICK UP YOUR PENCIL, PAINTBRUSH OR MOUSE AND YOU GIVE FREE REIN TO YOUR CREATIVE IMPULSES. BUT... DO YOU USE PERSPECTIVE? THE POSSIBILITIES ARE TWO, OR RATHER FOUR:

(a) YOU'VE NEVER HEARD OF IT AND YOU DON'T USE IT;

(b) YOU KNOW WHAT IT IS BUT YOU DON'T LIKE IT AND NEVER USE IT;

(c) YOU USE IT UNAWARES;

(d) YOU USE IT, AND KNOW ALL ABOUT IT.

THOSE LUCKY PEOPLE WHO BELONG TO THE SECOND AND FOURTH CATEGORIES CAN SKIP THE NEXT BIT. AS FOR THE OTHERS, DON'T WORRY, YOU'RE IN GOOD COMPANY: ALL THE SO-CALLED 'PRIMITIVE' CULTURES, MANY HIGHLY DEVELOPED CULTURES SUCH AS THOSE OF ANCIENT EGYPT AND CRETE, THE ART OF INDIA, ISLAMIC ART, PRE-RENAISSANCE EUROPEAN ART (NOT TO MENTION THE ART OF LITTLE CHILDREN) PAY NO ATTENTION TO PERSPECTIVE, EXCEPT IN RARE INSTANCES. TO GIVE A CLASSIC EXAMPLE: IN ANCIENT EGYPTIAN PAINTINGS THE FIGURES ARE SHOWN WITH THE HEAD AND LEGS IN PROFILE, BUT WITH THE EYES AND TORSO SEEN FROM THE FRONT. AND MODERN ARTISTS? MANY OF THEM BELONG TO THE SECOND CATEGORY, THAT IS TO SAY THEY KNOW WHAT PERSPECTIVE IS, BUT FOR REASONS OF THEIR OWN THEY IGNORE IT. AND OTHERS REALLY DON'T NEED IT AT ALL, BECAUSE THEIR WORK IS ABSTRACT.

BUT WHAT EXACTLY IS PERSPECTIVE? IT IS A METHOD WHICH ALLOWS US TO REPRODUCE OBJECTS AND SPACES IN THREE DIMENSIONS (LENGTH, WIDTH AND DEPTH) ON A TWO-DIMENSIONAL SURFACE (LENGTH AND WIDTH ONLY), OR ON A VERY SHALLOW THREE-DIMENSIONAL SURFACE SUCH AS A BAS-RELIEF. IN OTHER WORDS IT ALLOWS US TO CREATE THE OPTICAL ILLUSION OF SPACE AND VOLUME BY REPRESENTING THEM AS THEY APPEAR FROM A PRECISE VIEWPOINT.

There are various types of perspective, but they are all based on the idea of the 'vanishing point.' If you look around you, you will notice that the further away objects are, the smaller they appear to be, and that parallel lines and surfaces converge towards a point very (or rather infinitely) far away—the vanishing point. When parallel lines are represented as converging, we call it linear perspective: this may be central or oblique, depending on how many vanishing points are used (one in the first case, two or more in the second), and is characteristic of Western painting from the Renaissance onwards. We call it parallel perspective when the parallel lines remain parallel; this kind of perspective represents scenes as though they were seen from above, and is characteristic of Chinese painting.

The mathematical laws of perspective established by the Greeks and Romans were forgotten during the Middle Ages. They were rediscovered in the early 15th century by Filippo Brunelleschi, who found out all about vanishing points and realised that the apparent size of an object is inversely proportionate to its distance from the spectator. Brunelleschi applied these principles to two demonstration panels, unfortunately lost, which showed streets and buildings in Florence. The same principles were used by Masaccio (see for example his "Trinity" fresco in Santa Maria Novella), and within a very short time were all over the place: thousands and thousands of paintings have backgrounds with interiors or exteriors shown in perspective.

Brunelleschi's discoveries were explained by Leon Battista Alberti (who also worked at Santa Maria Novella as an architect) in his treatise "On Painting" (De Pictura, 1436), which is the first systematic treatment of the subject and is dedicated, not surprisingly, to Brunelleschi.

Linear perspective dominated the art of painting until the end of the 19th century. Then along came Paul Cézanne and the Cubists... but that's another story, isn't it?

CRAFTSMANSHIP & RENAISSANCE

THE OPIFICIO DELLE PIETRE DURE

he Princes' Chapel sure is amazing. It must be awfully hard to cut stone like that."

"As a matter of fact, the Italian expression for semi-precious stone is *pietre dure*, which literally means 'hard stones.' They don't call 'em that for nothing."

"Not like rocks in general are known for their softness…"

"True, but smooth, coloured stone like that: you can't even *scratch* it with a regular hammer and chisel. You need special techniques to work it properly."

"Such as?"

"I think I'll let my friend Franco explain it to you."

Franco was a lanky character, tall and completely bald. An unlit *toscano* cigar dangled in his mouth throughout their visit. He started off by explaining that *opificio* means workshop, and that the Opificio delle Pietre Dure was where unfinished or discarded projects in semi-precious stone used to be kept. The latter would then be disassembled piece by piece for reuse.

"Our story begins around the time of Grand Duke Francesco de' Medici—the Studiolo fellow. He inherited his family's love of semi-precious stone, and was anxious to rediscover the secret to working it: the techniques used

VINCENT VAN GOGH, OIL ON CANVAS? WRONG
SEMI-PRECIOUS-STONE INLAY BY GEROLAMO DELLA VALL

THE OPIFICIO DELLE PIETRE DURE

THE SEMI-PRECIOUS STONES USED FOR INLAYS—IN ITALIAN, 'COMMESSI', WHICH MEANS PUT TOGETHER, UNITED, JOINED UP—WERE OF MANY KINDS: VARIOUS TYPES OF QUARTZ (ROCK CRYSTAL, AMETHYST, PINK OR BLUE QUARTZ), CHALCEDONY (ONYX, AGATE) AND JASPER. SOME OF THE SEMI-PRECIOUS STONES CAME FROM DISTANT LANDS—FROM THE FAR EAST OR FROM THE AMERICAS. THE TECHNIQUE, DEVELOPED IN FLORENCE IN THE 16TH CENTURY, INVOLVED CUTTING THE STONES INTO SHAPES AND FITTING THEM TOGETHER ON TOP OF A DRAWING SUPPLIED BY THE ARTIST. THE CRAFTSMAN TRIED TO MAKE AN EXACT COPY OF THIS DRAWING, EVEN REPRODUCING THE SLIGHTEST GRADATIONS OF COLOUR. THE INLAY SHOWN HERE, NOW IN THE UFFIZI GALLERY, WAS MADE BY CRISTOFANO GAFFURI TO A DESIGN BY JACOPO LIGOZZI, AND SHOWS THE PORT OF LIVORNO (OR LEGHORN), FOUNDED BY GRAND DUKE COSIMO I. HE HAD BECOME INCREASINGLY WORRIED BECAUSE THE PORT OF PISA HAD BEEN SILTING UP AND GETTING FURTHER AND FURTHER FROM THE SEA. LIVORNO, THE HOME OF A DELICIOUS FISH SOUP CALLED 'CACCIUCCO,' SOON BECAME A HIGHLY IMPORTANT COMMERCIAL CENTRE. GRAND DUKE FERDINANDO I GRANTED THE CITY A SPECIAL CHARTER WHICH GUARANTEED RELIGIOUS LIBERTY, THEREBY ATTRACTING NOT ONLY ENGLISH AND FRENCH PROTESTANTS BUT ALSO MANY PROSPEROUS JEWISH MERCHANTS.

by the Egyptians, Greeks and Romans were all lost during the Middle Ages. Francesco summoned the finest stonecutters and jewellers to Florence, and put them together in the same room. Each had their own speciality, but they worked in close collaboration. These men deserve most of the credit for the rebirth of this exceptional art form. Francesco wasn't going to let a little thing like money stand in his way. He ordered rare and costly minerals not only from grand-ducal territories like the island of Elba, but from distant countries like Persia and India as well. The artisans started producing fabulous cups and vases in a variety of shapes and materials; they carved the stone, melted the metals, experimented with alchemy… They created some extraordinary pieces, but it took them a heck of a long time to get anything done: in part, because the projects themselves were so complicated; in part, because the artisans weren't exactly masters in time management…"

"Are you saying they were goof-offs?"

"You could put it that way. They played practical jokes on each other and squandered a lot of time. After

DON GIOVANNI DE' MEDICI & MATTEO NIGETTI, DESIGN FOR THE ALTAR IN THE PRINCES' CHAPEL

Francesco died, though, his brother Ferdinando stepped in and changed all that. He was an efficiency buff: he moved the workshop to the Uffizi, close to home, so that he could personally oversee each phase of production. From then on, the Opificio dealt mostly in decorative household goods: cabinets, boxes, tables that were used by the court or given away to prestigious guests. Anyway, these were the artists that decorated the Princes' Chapel. The hunt for rare stone stimulated trade with Spain and Portugal, who were extracting precious minerals from mines in their American colonies. This research even led to the discovery of unexplored territories!"

"Cool!"

"Ferdinando actively supported the expeditions of daring explorers. What's more, he passed a grand-ducal decree forbidding his subjects from trading or selling semi-precious stone behind his back. He wanted it all! The penalty was ten years of rowing in the royal galleys."

There were all manner of things in the Opificio museum, including table tops and pictures that resembled elaborate, stone jigsaw puzzles… Philip was naturally struck by the little model of the Princes' Chapel; next to it were decorated panels prepared for the mausoleum, but never used.

"What a difference: the models painted on wood and canvas are all faded or damaged, while the actual thing in semi-precious stone is still in perfect condition!"

The craftsmen's tools and workbenches were found on the upper floor. By examining the projects displayed in the various stages of production, Philip saw how the different kinds of stones (agate, carnelian, jasper…) were being worked. A glass panel ran along the entire length of the wall, protecting a huge sampling of multicoloured stones, all of them… cut in slices. These enabled the workmen to choose the colours that best suited their particular project.

"The stones have curious names that often hint at their origin: touchstone of Flanders, lined stone of the Arno, antique black of Aquitaine… But it wasn't all just a matter of interior design: they were believed to have magical powers."

"Such as?"

"Well, emerald was supposed to jog the memory, ruby was good for the health and protection against poison, sapphire had soothing properties…"

"Like the mood-changing machine in *Blade Runner*," the archaeologist added. "A rock a day keeps the doctor away!"

"Putting a diamond in your mouth was supposed to quench your appetite."

"I'd spend less than I do at a restaurant," Uncle Charlie sighed, casting a baleful look at his nephew.

PIAZZA SANTISSIMA ANNUNZIATA

They were headed towards Piazza Santissima Annunziata. Charles was explaining how there had been a children's hospital in Florence as early as the Middle Ages.

"The one known as the Bigallo Confraternity is there next to the Duomo: you remember that little white marble loggia with the two arches? Anyway, they weren't really hospitals in the modern sense of the word. Of course, they treated disease, too: infant mortality was very high back then. But they mostly served as orphanages. This one here in Piazza Santissima Annunziata is the most famous: it's called the *Spedale degli Innocenti*, or Hospital of the Innocents."

"Nice piazza. It looks so… orderly!"

"The hospital and square were designed by the same architect: an old buddy of ours…"

GIAMBOLOGNA & PIETRO TACCA,
EQUESTRIAN STATUE OF FERDINANDO I DE' MEDICI

"Arnolf… No, wait a minute… Filippo!"

"Bravo! With this project Brunelleschi virtually 'invented' Renaissance architecture, applying lessons he had learned by studying ancient Roman construction. You see, town squares weren't usually planned. They just sort of 'happened' spontaneously: at an intersection, around a well, in front of a church… This one, in contrast, was all mapped out on the drafting table: the existing jumble of orchards and shacks was to be substituted by a spacious and gracious piazza. He only got as far as the galleries in his lifetime, though."

THE SPEDALE DEGLI INNOCENTI

"High up between the grey arches there are tondo decorations with a blue background. Those are infants in swaddling clothes: they called them 'innocents'…"

"Like in the famous 'Slaughter of the Innocents'…"

"Like Herod's slaughter, exactly. The loggia design was revolutionary because each element had a fixed and predetermined measure in precise relationship to all the others. They hadn't done anything like that for centuries."

"What's so special about it?"

"For example, take the arches that divide the naves of the large Gothic churches in Florence. Each one is different from the next. The first might be thirteen metres across, let's say, the second, sixteen and the third, fifteen. That's because medieval men weren't particularly worried about uniformity. Brunelleschi's arches, on the other hand, are all identical. What's more, the *width* of each arch is equal to the *height* of the column and the *depth* of the arcade. That way, the various elements—both individually *and* taken as a whole—break up the space

into precise geometric patterns. The sense of order that you picked up on is created by this proportion game. The naked eye isn't able to measure a single object to the metre, much less so to the centimetre, but you instinctively *feel* the relationships between the measurements and the sense of equilibrium that they create. That was one of classical architecture's most important lessons, and Brunelleschi learned it so well that he seasoned the main course—symmetry, that is—with ancient ingredients: columns, tondi, Corinthian capitals…"

"What was that square window inside the loggia for?"

"When a woman had a baby that she couldn't keep because she was poor or… for her own reasons, if you catch my drift… she would bring it here under the loggia. A wheel stuck out from the wall under the window: you'd put the baby on it, spin it around and ring the doorbell. That way the staff would know that another guest had arrived. It was sort of like a revolving door."

"And what would they do with these little 'innocents'?"

"They didn't have co-ed classes in those days. Filippo designed a square cloister for the boys, called the 'men's cloister;' and another, longer one for the girls, called the 'women's cloister.' Infants were entrusted to nannies who looked after them, changed their swaddling clothes and nursed them. They always hired healthy, plump women for this line of work—preferably blond. I wonder why…"

"Come on: everybody knows that Babies Prefer Blondes."

"Another crack like that and you're on the next plane home!"

"I wouldn't dream of it."

"They kept a close eye out for cavities, to avoid the risk of infection. They used cow milk, too, served in the ancestor of the baby bottle: a glass bottle with a nipple made out of animal gut. The Silk Guild financed the Hospital, and saw to it that the children received an education. The boys learned how to raise the silkworms and weave fabric, the girls learned how to embroider."

"Child labour!"

"I know. But at least they learned a trade. Nowadays, on the other hand…"

MEDICI-RICCARDI PALACE

THE HISTORY OF A MANSION

ncle Charlie was seated on the bed, leafing through dog-eared travel guides in various languages. He looked up as Philip entered the room, comic book in hand.

"Listen, uncle, I was just wondering… Hold it right there: you're *busted*, Mister Know-it-all! Cramming for your next exam?"

"Don't be silly. I was just checking… a date."

"In five different books?"

"Sure. It's called 'verification'."

"Mmm… We'll let it go this time. Anyway, I was wondering where the Medici kept their deposit."

"What?"

"You know, like Uncle Scrooge… the house, the office, the place where they saved their first gold coin…"

"Their mansion! If you have the patience to wait until tomorrow…"

The next day, the two were in Via Cavour—formerly Via Larga—right in front of Cosimo the Elder's general headquarters.

"It's known as the Medici-Riccardi Palace. The Riccardi family bought it in 1670 and added onto it. Then they sold it in the early 1800s to the grand-ducal government. But let's start at the beginning."

"Brunelleschi, as usual?"

THE HISTORY OF A MANSION

"Almost. Brunelleschi presented Cosimo with an extravagant design. Boy, it was big: an imposing mansion with its very own piazza connecting it to the church of San Lorenzo."

"And?"

"And Cosimo knew better than that. He didn't want to make the other merchants jealous, you see. So he opted for a less, shall we say, ostentatious solution."

"No deposit on the top of a hill."

"No. Cosimo was a successful entrepreneur, but he still wasn't the city's ruler. That's why he approved Michelozzo's less-grandiose design. Michelozzo was one of Brunelleschi's followers."

"It's doesn't look much like the tower-houses, or even Palazzo Davanzati. It's massive, but it doesn't have that fortress look."

"In fact, the Florentines of the time must have been pretty astonished. It's wider than it is tall, and there's an elegant roof instead of the usual crenellation on top. The outer walls are faced in *pietra forte* and divided into three horizontal strips, one for each floor. On the ground floor, the stone blocks are rough-hewn and protrude from the wall. They stick out less on the first floor, and are practically smooth by the top…"

"That lightens up the façade and gives it a lofty look."

"Won't be long before *you're* the one giving the tours around here. The two large windows at the corner were added by Michelangelo to close off the loggia. It was a bit too open and thus risky in case of popular uprising against the Medici. The other windows on the ground floor are small and high, like those of the tower-houses, while those on the upper floors are much bigger."

"That must be why this place seems less gloomy than medieval houses."

"And it served as the model for other mansions. As usual, the wealthy families tried to outdo each other, but now the winning criteria was not height, but comfort. *And* the extravagance of the parties inside. As far as parties were concerned, the Medici were second to none. Come, let's take a look at the garden!"

LORENZO & CLARICE

"This was the setting for some magnificent parties... and some pretty fine feasts, as well," Uncle Charlie continued, winking at his nephew. "One of the most famous was held for the wedding of Lorenzo the Magnificent, Cosimo the Elder's grandson. Just picture bejewelled ladies exchanging witty remarks between dances; servants running here and there in a frenzy, periodically tripping over the ornamental plants; the gentlemen—nobility, merchants, often both—talking business and poetry. The light shimmers off the damask of the gowns, the courtyard echoes with music and sonnets, a veritable labyrinth of meaningful glances and murmurs... but, there, I'm getting carried away again."

"I was about to say."

"Fine. She was standing to one side of the courtyard: Clarice Orsini, a haughty Roman girl of noble birth. Red hair, fair complexion, a bit on the plump side..."

"White dress?"

"That actually wasn't customary back then. Wedding dresses were usually some intense colour: bright green or expensive red."

"And Lorenzo?" Philip prodded, enjoying himself.

"Down at the other end of the courtyard, looking pensive."

"Handsome?"

"Not really, but with a charismatic charm. He was wearing an oriental outfit, 'Turk-style,' very fashionable. It was the first time that he had ever laid eyes on his betrothed—that was normal, in those days—but his eyes were hungering for another…"

"Just what we needed—a Renaissance soap opera."

"Men *have and have always had identical passions*, as Machiavelli used to say."

"But we're sinking to the trashy gossip level here! Go on, who *was* this other woman?"

"Her name was Lucrezia Donati. They continued their secret love affair right up until Lorenzo died. How romantic… Let's go upstairs: I want to show you something special."

"Forget archaeology! I mean, you should write romance novels."

"There's still time. I'd earn a lot more money, too."

SELF-PORTRAIT OF BENOZZO GOZZOLI! AND THERE'S ANOTHER ONE A BIT LOWER DOWN.

THE CHAPEL OF THE MAGI

A broad staircase led them to the 'special something' that Charles was talking about: the mansion's private chapel. It wasn't hard to tell what was so special about it: on the walls, an elaborate procession of knights wound its way through a lush landscape full of plants and animals.

"The fresco depicts the cavalcade of the Magi. The knight with the crown is supposed to be Lorenzo."

"He's not so bad-looking after all."

"Actually, we're not sure that it's him. Some say the figure is the personification of Youth, or Europe, or that it represents an abstract ideal of the prince. Nevertheless, a description of Lorenzo in that very outfit *was* found in an old chronicle. It's a fairly simple get-up: tights with a double-sleeved jacket. But the fabric is richly embroidered with boughs and interlocking patterns: fish scales on his belly, bat wings and peacock feathers on his chest."

"Who's the artist?"

"Benozzo Gozzoli, who incidentally included a self-portrait in the scene and signed it in gold on his cap. Poor fellow: as you can see, there aren't

THE YOUNGEST OF THE THREE KINGS
(LORENZO THE MAGNIFICENT?)

116

BENOZZO'S THIRD SELF-PORTRAIT: SO MANY PEOPLE OUT THERE, HE WAS RUNNING OUT OF FACES!

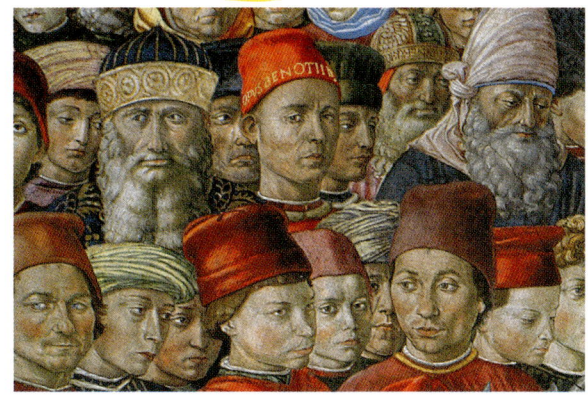

any windows in here, and he had to paint by torchlight. Restorers have shown that he used different techniques according to the effects he wanted to create: fresco for the faces, and colours mixed with egg—and therefore a little more dense—to give light to the clothing…"

LORENZO THE MAGNIFICENT, REALISTIC VERSION: WATCH OUT FOR 'THE NOSE!'

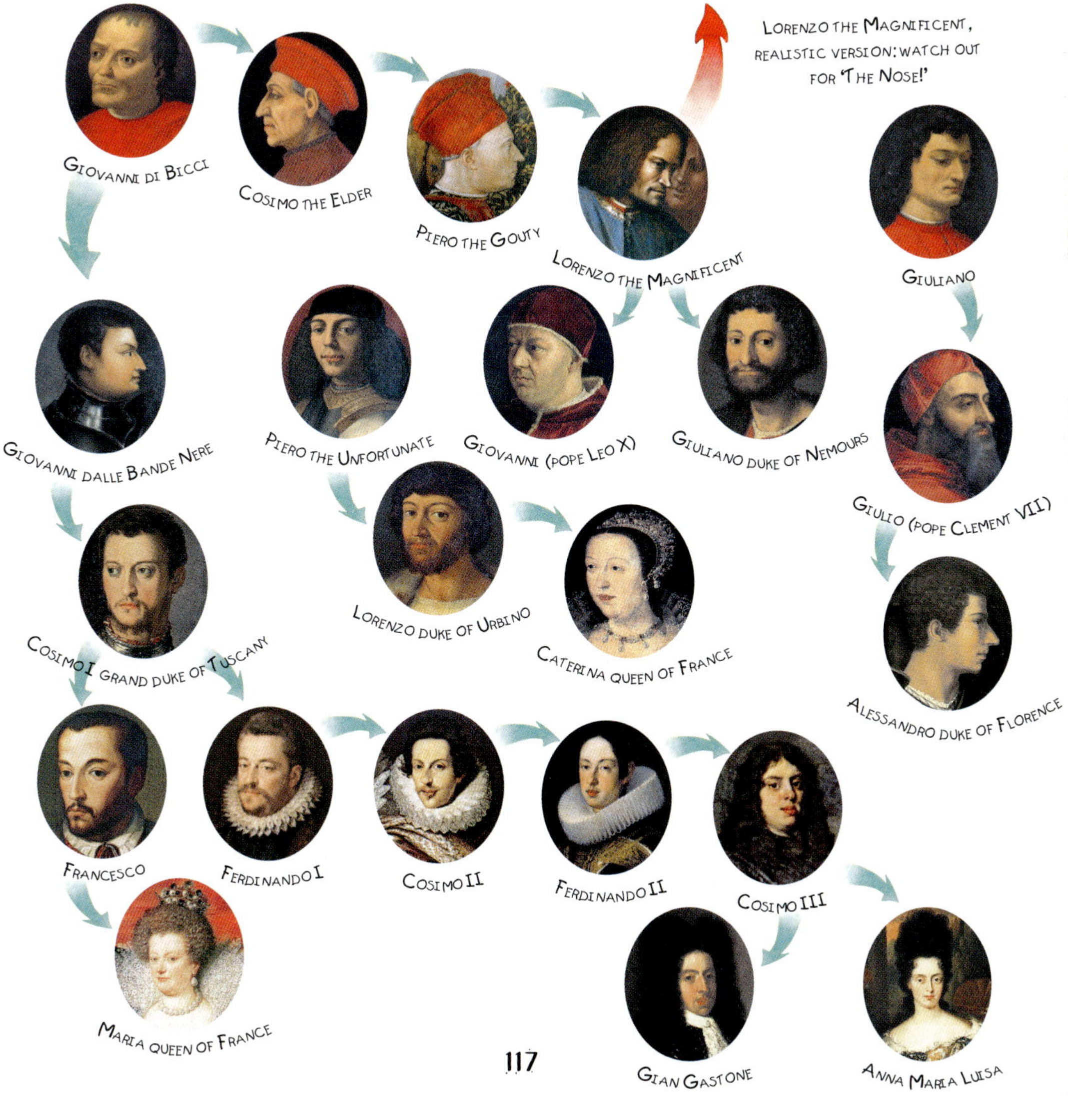
GIOVANNI DI BICCI
COSIMO THE ELDER
PIERO THE GOUTY
LORENZO THE MAGNIFICENT
GIULIANO
GIOVANNI DALLE BANDE NERE
PIERO THE UNFORTUNATE
GIOVANNI (POPE LEO X)
GIULIANO DUKE OF NEMOURS
GIULIO (POPE CLEMENT VII)
COSIMO I GRAND DUKE OF TUSCANY
LORENZO DUKE OF URBINO
CATERINA QUEEN OF FRANCE
ALESSANDRO DUKE OF FLORENCE
FRANCESCO
FERDINANDO I
COSIMO II
FERDINANDO II
COSIMO III
MARIA QUEEN OF FRANCE
GIAN GASTONE
ANNA MARIA LUISA

BARGELLO & STIBBERT MUSEUMS

HISTORY OF THE BARGELLO

heir decision was made at the Roman theatre in Fiesole. On the large screen in front of them, a motley band of medieval characters pummelled each other with bludgeons and swords.

"Florence has a little bit of everything," Philip commented during the intermission, "but what it *doesn't* have is a good old-fashioned castle like the one in the movie. Even Palazzo Vecchio: it looks good enough from the outside, then you enter the courtyard and there's the quaint little column here, the dainty little fountain there… You don't get that good, gloomy atmosphere."

"The best that we can offer…" Giulia began. The next morning they were standing outside the Bargello National Museum. For centuries this sober little castle had witnessed the tormented roller-coaster of Florentine politics.

"Today this building hosts one of the most important sculpture collections in the world. There are statues from the Middle Ages and Renaissance; objects in gold, ceramic, enamel, ivory and bronze; arms and jewellery. Once upon a time, however, the building served as a prison."

"I remember you telling me about it when we were taking the tower-house tour. Let's have a look."

Enclosed by a tall, partially crenellated wall, the courtyard met Philip's high expectations. Coats of arms were plastered into the walls, their colours long since faded away. They represented the *podestà* and judges who ruled from the building for nearly two hundred years.

"During the 1800s the entire building and courtyard were restored according to the neo-medieval taste of the time. The statues under the portico were brought in from various buildings throughout the city."

DONATELLO'S "ST GEORGE"

They entered the first room of the museum, which originally served as the general council's meeting chambers. Philip was in for his first surprise. The original of Orsanmichele's *St George* was situated high up on the back wall, surrounded by a variety of Renaissance sculptures.

"*St George* definitely stands out," Giulia observed. "He's the room's star attraction, and not only because he's located in a priv-

ileged position in a specially designed tabernacle. He seems to give out an enormous physical and mental energy, concentration and strength put together."

"Yes, a real hero," Philip agreed, enjoying his new-found role as art critic. "The frowning forehead, the determined but calm expression, the slightly spread legs… He's sure of himself, and isn't going to give an inch. He's like Clint Eastwood in those Sergio Leone spaghetti westerns."

Giulia and Uncle Charlie chuckled appreciatively. "A real Renaissance man," the archaeologist added, "because he knows what he wants and is determined to get it. But you already said it all… Remember Lorenzo's wife, Clarice Orsini? She was sure to have a nuptial chest like the one under the *St George*."

"What's a nuptial chest?"

"The chest where a bride's dowry was stored. This one's decorated with a scene from St John the Baptist Day. Most Florentine weddings took place that time of year: that way the guests could enjoy the nice weather and the festivities organized for the holiday. The cornice is decorated with embossed, gilded lilies. In between the emblems of the bride and groom's families, you see the procession of the *gonfaloni*, or standards. The parade took place every year in celebration of the patron saint's holiday. Behind the crowd of merrymakers, you see the unmistakable outline of the baptistery, welcoming the knights' procession with open doors."

"Why isn't the lid painted?"

"It might have been, originally, and later replaced because of old age or damage. Or maybe it was once lined with fabric."

"Here's another one of Donatello's bronzes: the *David*," Giulia declared. "He's resting his foot on Goliath's head, but it's hard to believe that a delicate boy like

ABOVE THE DOOR OF THE BAPTISTERY YOU CAN SEE THE "BAPTISM OF CHRIST" BY TINO DI CAMAINO, NOW IN THE OPERA DEL DUOMO MUSEUM

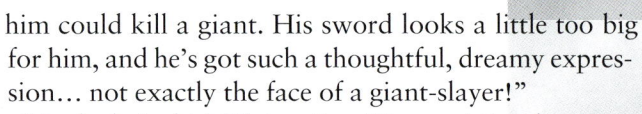

THE "ST JOHN" ATTRIBUTED TO DESIDERIO DA SETTIGNANO

him could kill a giant. His sword looks a little too big for him, and he's got such a thoughtful, dreamy expression… not exactly the face of a giant-slayer!"

"And who's this? Wait… *San Giovanni*. St John. He looks like a wreck, all skin and bones!"

"I'd like to see *you* after years of fasting in the desert! He stayed alive by eating locusts and wild honey."

"Not a good idea: you know what I'm like when my blood sugar's low. And while we're on the subject…"

"Take it easy. Let's finish up here first."

OTHER ROOMS

"Speaking of skin and bones, did you know that there was a time when Florence was famous for its anatomical studies? Specialized doctors dissected corpses in front of artists who followed the entire procedure, drawing the various phases. The artists came to know the human body right down to the last little muscle: that's why they were so good at reproducing it in their painting and sculpture."

"You're wrecking my appetite with all this corpse talk!"
"Impossible!"

"Speaking of realism…" Giulia intervened, "take a look at that bust of Niccolò da Uzzano. He was a Florentine scholar and, as you can see, not exactly handsome. Look at the care Donatello took in modelling him: wrinkles around the mouth, sunken eyes… even his Adam's apple and scraggly whiskers! He did it in three pieces with casts taken directly from his subject's face."

"Look, Charlie, a chessboard!" Philip exclaimed, entering the Carrand room. "With a backgammon set on the flip side!"

"It's actually a travel chess set from the Middle Ages," Charles corrected him tenderly. "It folds up into a carrying case. The original checkers and chess pieces have

BECAUSE OF ITS GREAT PURCHASING POWER AND WIDE CIRCULATION THE FLORIN HAS BEEN CALLED "THE DOLLAR OF THE MIDDLE AGES"

been lost, but in compensation there are some beautiful ones in the display case here: some are carved in ivory, and not just elephant but *walrus* tusk!"

"The border's decorated with damsels wearing pointy caps like Gandalf or Merlin might have worn. Now those were the days: knights, duels... and feasts!"

"You've got a one-track mind! All right, grab yourself some antique flatware. Back when other people were still eating with their hands, the Florentines were already using the knife and fork. Not all of them, though. Those ewers were used to pour perfumed water into the diners' hands, and the basins served to collect the overflow."

"So where did they hide the medieval dining room?"

"Copy that, loud and clear. Let's go."

As they were leaving the Bargello, Uncle Charlie launched into a lecture. "I think you should know that in those days, chess rules were a bit different. The queen and the bishop both moved diagonally, one and two squares respectively. There was no such thing as the castle, and the opening pawn was only allowed to advance one square, not two. In compensation, victory was declared when your adversary was stalemated, or when the king was his only piece left on the board. In 1497, in Salamanca..."

As Charles droned on about the publication of a fundamental text on chess openings, Philip and Giulia exchanged glances. Their expression, alas, was not that of St George.

'BURGONET' WITH EAGLE'S'S HEAD

The Stibbert Museum & Gardens

The three caught a bus that crossed the ring roads and brought them outside the historic centre. They got off at the foot of a hill, and noticed one of Florence's most striking characteristics: that you can move from urban to rural in a matter of minutes, particularly if you follow the north–south axis running perpendicular to the Arno River. A five-minute walk (three minutes uphill and two to catch their breath and admire the dome in the distance) brought them from the bus stop to the gate of the Stibbert Museum.

"What does 'Stibbert' mean?"

"That was the last name of the man who owned the house: Frederick—or Federico, in Italian—Stibbert. The street is even named after him. He was born in Florence to an English father and Florentine mother. His father's family had administered some territory in the East Indies—colonies, you know—and when his parents died, Frederick was left with a very sizeable inheritance."

"Lucky him!"

"What do you think he did with it?"

"Put it in a supersafe."

"Not on your life! He dedicated himself to his favourite hobby: collecting antique arms. When he died, he left the house, garden, and fabulous arms collection to the British government. They, in turn, kindly gave it over to the city of Florence. Let's go!"

124

"As you can see," Giulia said, "the arms are not simply 'displayed.' In order to create a more realistic effect, Stibbert arranged his collection on manikins and horses made out of plaster. When he had guests over for dinner, he would take them on a tour of the house: they were all shocked silly, of course, and he was happy as a clam."

"That must have been a real kick: open a door to go to the bathroom and out pops an armed knight!"

"Exactly: if they have that power over those of us who are used to special effects, imagine what it must have been like for people back then."

125

Giulia pointed out that the coats of armour worn by the infantry were light and flexible, while those worn by the knights were rigid and extremely heavy. The parade armour could be identified by gold decorations on the breastplate.

"Look, this one was engraved with an image of Jesus to protect the warrior who wore it… And now, medieval aficionado, get ready!"

They entered a large room. Before them, a shiny, magnificent procession of knights—on horseback, obviously—clothed and armed to the hilt.

"These are Italian, German and Turkish knights. The Germans wore the striped armour, and the visor of their helmets was the shape of a bear or lion. The Turks, for their part, had pointed boots and helmets, and instead of the cuirass wore coats of 'light' chain mail. What do you think? Doesn't it feel like we've gone back in time?"

"That, or to some good movie set."

"This room also holds the armour that Giovanni dalle Bande Nere was buried in. Giovanni was a great mercenary captain, and Grand Duke Cosimo I's father. There's so much on the walls it's hard to decide what to look at: swords, crossbows, bows, springals, halberds, guns…"

The visit continued in the ball room, where parties were hosted. In one of the rooms on the first floor, they came across the outfit that Napoleon was wearing when he was crowned King of Italy.

"If you were to write an adventure story, this would be the perfect place to be," Philip noted, examining a Japanese suit of armour. The mask looked squarely back at him with a ferocious expression.

"That's right. Especially writers like Salgari…"

"The one who wrote about Sandokan and the Black Corsair!"

"The very same. But maybe you didn't realize that although his stories were set in distant lands, and although he describes exotic places, customs, arms and clothing in minute detail… he never set foot outside of Italy."

"His details were a little *too* minute for my tastes," Uncle Charlie confessed. "I remember a scene where the hero is being chased by the bad guys: he escapes into a forest and trips over a root. Instead of continuing his story, Salgari goes into this whole discussion about the plant: such and such height, grows only in certain regions, used for such and such…"

After the ritual pit-stop in the museum cafe, they went out to the villa gardens. Philip was in for another treat: a tree-lined boulevard ended at a small lake with swans, ducks… and a small Egyptian temple on its banks.

"I must admit—surprises never end in this city."

THE DOMINICAN FRIAR GIROLAMO SAVONAROLA (FERRARA 1452-FLORENCE 1498)

IN A PORTRAIT BY FRA BARTOLOMEO (SAN MARCO MUSEUM)

SAN MARCO
& THE ACCADEMIA

THE CONVENT OF SAN MARCO

After all those knights and armour and whatnot, a peaceful convent is just what we need."

"Sounds good to me. We've been to mansions, churches, museums... but no convents so far."

"San Marco's not exactly your typical convent," Uncle Charlie began. "Don't expect white walls and modest chambers. This was a very important Dominican convent, financed by Cosimo de' Medici himself. The structure dates back to the end of the 1200s, but then Cosimo hired Michelozzo to make the facilities more functional, more in keeping with new trends in taste and thought."

"Michelozzo is the guy who did Palazzo Medici, right?"

"Exactly. Cosimo picked up all the expenses here: design, masonry, furnishing... And he entrusted the decoration of the most important rooms to a friar painter who actually lived in the convent. Pretty convenient, don't you think?"

"A friar painter?"

"His real name was Giovanni da Fiesole, but he was nicknamed 'Angelico' for the grace of his brushstroke and also for his goodness: in fact, the Church declared him *beatus*, or 'blessed.' The Dominican order was sophisticated and powerful, and befriending it was a brilliant political move on Cosimo's part. The work he sponsored there was great in terms of his public image: not coincidentally, the Medici family 'balls' can be found all over the place. Convents are very carefully ordered complexes. Each part is linked to the friars' rules or to a particular moment in their day, and nothing is left to chance. The cloister, for example, is an open area in the centre of the convent, and the loggia allows you to cross it even when it rains. The most important settings in the life of a friar all opened onto the

FRA ANGELICO

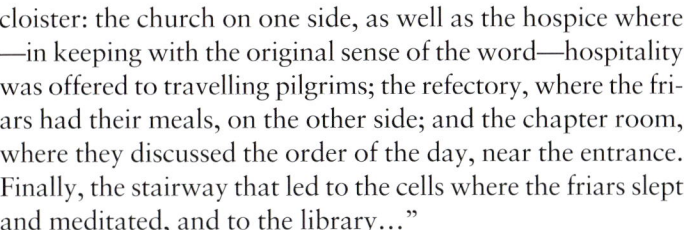

cloister: the church on one side, as well as the hospice where —in keeping with the original sense of the word—hospitality was offered to travelling pilgrims; the refectory, where the friars had their meals, on the other side; and the chapter room, where they discussed the order of the day, near the entrance. Finally, the stairway that led to the cells where the friars slept and meditated, and to the library…"

"Where they read…"

FRA ANGELICO

"…where they read, studied and wrote. There are various pieces by Fra Angelico in the hospice, all painted on wooden panels. They all treat religious themes, as you might expect— yet are very different in terms of form and style. You move from a gold-leafed, quite Gothic triptych to square panel paintings with a Renaissance feel: landscapes in the background and a less stylized, more natural arrangement of the figures… In that one, for example, the saints surrounding the Virgin Mary seem to be chatting among themselves. Some of the saints were particularly dear to the Medici: St Dominic, for example, wearing the black and white habit of his order and holding a lily in his hand; Peter, a Dominican martyr,

with blood on his head; St Lawrence, wearing a sumptuous red garment bordered in gold, and carrying the grate that he was martyred on; and finally Cosmas (that Cosimo was named after) and his brother Damian— two doctors who performed miracles. The Medici chose them as their patron saints."

"You make it sound almost trendy: saints of the season, spring-summer line, 1520…"

"Well, I wouldn't go that far, but yes: a saint that was

MARK
OHN
WRENCE

COSMAS & DAMIAN   DOMINIC   FRANCIS

PETER MARTYR

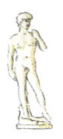

considered particularly important at one point in time might be put aside in favour of another, depending on the circumstances. Now let's get your professional opinion on that *Last Judgement* there."

"Paradise is full of colour, and there are some blessed little friars playing ring-around-the-rosy with the Good People and the angels. The damned are in hell, on the other hand, along with… popes and kings?"

"You can't judge a pope by his vestments, as some of the popes of the time just went to show. Look at how Angelico told the story of Jesus in those little panels. They were actually the doors of a precious cabinet that was subsequently dismantled."

"It's another example of what we were talking about at the baptistery and Santa Croce: the importance of images for people who didn't know how to read."

"In spite of the rather small format, it's easy to spot the perspective used on the buildings, the characters' details, and even the expressions on their faces! He was good, there's no denying it. Good with the small stuff—like the illuminated codices in the library on the next floor—good with the big stuff, like the *Crucifixion* in the chapter room."

The three took a timely break at the top of the stairs, admiring a wonderful *Annunciation* set in a cloister suspiciously similar to

the convent's. They then set off resolutely in the direction of the friars' cells, each of which housed its own fresco.

"The style here is simpler, and the colours less costly: blue and red are missing, to say nothing of gold. No frills, in keeping with the friars' frugal lifestyle. The older ones got to choose the subject they wanted on their walls, while youths had to be content with a Crucifixion or scenes of the Passion, designed to inspire and teach. Angelico really whipped them out, too: he could fresco a cell in less than a week!"

COSIMO THE ELDER SEEMS TO HAVE FELT VERY MUCH AT HOME AT SAN MARCO—IN FACT HE LIVED JUST ROUND THE CORNER, IN VIA LARGA. THIS IS HARDLY SURPRISING: WITH THE POPE'S APPROVAL HE GOT MICHELOZZO TO REBUILD THE CHURCH AND CONVENT OF THE DOMINICANS, WITH NO EXPENSE SPARED. AS A BONUS, HE FILLED THE FRIARS' LIBRARY WITH RARE AND VALUABLE MANUSCRIPTS, COLLECTED OR COPIED FOR HIM BY THE LEARNED NICCOLÒ NICCOLI (THEY LATER BECAME PART OF THE LAURENTIAN LIBRARY). IN EXCHANGE THE GENEROUS BANKER WAS ALLOWED TWO CELLS JUST FOR HIMSELF, SO THAT HE COULD PRAY AND MEDITATE WHENEVER HE FELT LIKE IT.

THE STORY OF A BLOCK OF MARBLE

As soon as they were done at San Marco, Philip and Charles made their way to the nearby Accademia. Giulia wasn't in the mood to wait in any more lines. She decided she had some things to take care of and excused herself.

"I can see her point," Uncle Charlie admitted, smoothing his beard, "but the giant can't wait."

FRA ANGELICO, "ANNUNCIATION"

131

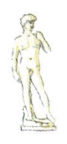

"The giant?"

"Michelangelo's *David*! That was what he was called in the chronicles of the day, and you'll soon see why. Meanwhile, I'll tell you the story. Once upon a time, there was block of marble from the Apuan Alps that was brought up the Arno to Florence. Some sculptor had wanted to make a giant out of it, but then for whatever reason got discouraged and gave up the idea. The marble had been sloppily hewn, and spent decades abandoned in the courtyard of the Opera del Duomo. Eventually, it fell into the hands of another sculptor, young and head-strong, who decided to make something of it. People shook their heads: 'It's useless,' they said. 'That other sculptor ruined it to the point that nothing good can ever come of it.' In order to escape gossip, and perhaps for good luck, the young sculptor had a sort of wooden fortress built around the block of marble, and he would close himself inside to work. The Florentines, busybodies by nature, couldn't bear the suspense: for two years, they tried in vain to peek inside to see how the work was coming along. But until the statue was finished, no one even caught a glimpse of it."

"Good for Michelangelo!"

"Vasari tells us that when Michelangelo was putting on the final touches, a bigwig stopped by and wanted to put his two-cents in. Looking at the sculpture from below, he declared that the nose was too big. That was nonsense, of course: he just couldn't see it properly from where he was standing. Michelangelo didn't want no trouble, and positioned himself between his foolish visitor and the

David: he pretended to trim the nose down—in fact he was just dropping marble dust that he had in this hand. 'Does it look all right now, sir?' he asked when he had finished. His guest happily exclaimed 'That's more like it! You've given him new life!' He thought he had contributed to the masterpiece, and all the while Michelangelo, being a

132

FURTHER MISFORTUNES OF THE "DAVID"!
IN 1527 A WOODEN BENCH CAME FLYING
OUT A WINDOW OF PALAZZO
VECCHIO (THE POLITICAL SITUATION WAS
A BIT JUMPY...) AND LANDED ON THE LEFT
ARM, BREAKING IT IN THREE PLACES—THE
FRAGMENTS WERE GATHERED UP AND
RESTORED BY VASARI.
IN 1544 ONE SHOULDER FELL OFF, AND
LANDED ON TOP OF A POOR FELLOW WHO
HAD COME TO TOWN TO ACCLAIM DUKE
COSIMO I. IN 1873 THE STATUE WAS
MOVED FROM PIAZZA DELLA SIGNORIA TO
THE ACCADEMIA; WHILE IT WAS WAITING
FOR ITS PLACE IN THE TRIBUNE IT WAS
LEFT WRAPPED UP FOR SO LONG THAT IT
DEVELOPED MEASLES (THE AIR COULDN'T
GET TO IT, SO THE MARBLE BECAME
STAINED WITH BLOTCHES OF MOULD). IN
1992 A LUNATIC SMASHED HIS BIG TOE
WITH A HAMMER.

MICHELANGELO'S "DAVID"

prankster by nature, was stringing him along… by the nose."

"So did the Florentines like it?"

"As soon as statue was uncovered, it was much admired by artists and population alike. But it also attracted jealousy and criticism. Let's just say that from the start, it was both loved and hated. There was also much discussion as to where it should be put. In the end they opted for the Piazza della Signoria, the heart of the city, and Michelangelo's location of choice. The statue was situated next to the main entrance of Palazzo Vecchio, where the brown *pietra forte* would bring out the white of the marble. But it was no small job to move it, being more than four metres tall, and some kind of heavy. With a little help from his friends, Michelangelo built a sort of train-car that moved down specially built tracks, drawn by teams of oxen. The 'voyage' lasted a week! The statue, wrapped up so that no one could see it, was guarded night and day. Nevertheless, a couple of jerks found a way to throw some rocks at it, and spent a week in the cooler for vandalism."

"The usual hooligans."

Their turn had finally arrived, and the two made their impatient way into the hall of the *David*.

MICHELANGELO'S "DAVID"

"8 September 1504…"

"The feast of Our Lady, if I'm not mistaken."

133

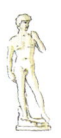

"That's right. On 8 September, the sculpture made its public debut. The people crammed into the square were amazed by the beauty of the nude. Moreover, this *David* was a true novelty. You remember the one by Donatello that we saw at the Bargello? Very young, big sword, Goliath's head underfoot... Now look at this one: robust, vigorous, nude as the heroes and athletes of antiquity, his gaze intelligent and courageous, a look of self-confidence, great moral and physical strength... For these very qualities, and for its being right outside the government seat, the Florentines promptly chose him as symbol of civic virtues, a bulwark against the enemies of liberty."

"But... where's Goliath's head?"

"Can't see it, because this David is shown the instant *before* throwing the rock that felled the giant. Hold on a minute. Look, try putting yourself in his position."

"No way, not in front of these people!"

"They're all busy taking pictures... Now, if you spread your legs a little and put all the weight of your body on your right leg, you'll see that the left knee naturally bends forward a little—a precarious balance that also causes your shoulder to lift..."

"Let's see here..."

"Now move your left hand toward your shoulder as if you were going to grab your slingshot."

"What were they like back in those days?"

"They would put a rock in a leather strap that was spun around to give it momentum. Pretend you have a rock in your right hand, turn your wrist and move your left leg forward... That's it. Perfect."

Applause suddenly rang out from a group of tourists gathered around the statue, accompanied by flashes.

"How embarrassing," Philip muttered under his breath.

"On the contrary," his uncle reassured him. "You gave a perfect demonstration. Are you comfortable?"

"No, thank you! My wrist hurts, and it's hard to keep my balance."

"But if you rest all your weight on the ball of your left foot, you'll find your chest twisting in such a way that it would seem natural to launch the rock

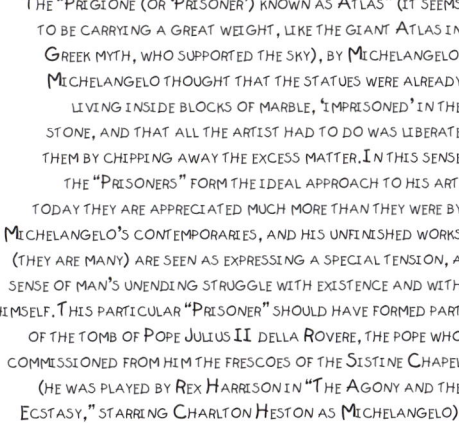

at the poor devil in front of you. Let's walk around the statue and appreciate its movements and expression—or, rather, expressions."

"That's strange. He seems to change position depending on your point of view, like in a movie sequence. But the proportions are a little strange: both his head and hands look too big for his body."

"There's a reason for that. The exaggerated proportions were intended to draw attention to the parts of the body linked to thought and action. It's a trick to make him easily recognizable as David; to say nothing of the slingshot, stone and look of concentration."

"Just like in the comic books: Spiderman's web, the costume…"

"That way you know immediately who he is and what he's doing."

"The guy's got class," Philip conceded, taking one last look at the masterpiece. "Which is more than I can say for most of the junk they hawk at the tourist stands!"

THE "PRIGIONE (OR 'PRISONER') KNOWN AS ATLAS" (IT SEEMS TO BE CARRYING A GREAT WEIGHT, LIKE THE GIANT ATLAS IN GREEK MYTH, WHO SUPPORTED THE SKY), BY MICHELANGELO. MICHELANGELO THOUGHT THAT THE STATUES WERE ALREADY LIVING INSIDE BLOCKS OF MARBLE, 'IMPRISONED' IN THE STONE, AND THAT ALL THE ARTIST HAD TO DO WAS LIBERATE THEM BY CHIPPING AWAY THE EXCESS MATTER. IN THIS SENSE THE "PRISONERS" FORM THE IDEAL APPROACH TO HIS ART: TODAY THEY ARE APPRECIATED MUCH MORE THAN THEY WERE BY MICHELANGELO'S CONTEMPORARIES, AND HIS UNFINISHED WORKS (THEY ARE MANY) ARE SEEN AS EXPRESSING A SPECIAL TENSION, A SENSE OF MAN'S UNENDING STRUGGLE WITH EXISTENCE AND WITH HIMSELF. THIS PARTICULAR "PRISONER" SHOULD HAVE FORMED PART OF THE TOMB OF POPE JULIUS II DELLA ROVERE, THE POPE WHO COMMISSIONED FROM HIM THE FRESCOES OF THE SISTINE CHAPEL (HE WAS PLAYED BY REX HARRISON IN "THE AGONY AND THE ECSTASY," STARRING CHARLTON HESTON AS MICHELANGELO).

THE MUSEUM OF THE HISTORY OF SCIENCE

ASTROLABES & ARMILLARY SPHERES

ops, I almost forgot. Before I left, my father—you know how he is, obsessed with technology and all that… He said I simply *must* see the Science Museum, where they keep that enormous armadillary sphere."

"I don't know about the armadillo, but the armillary sphere is there for real, and it's a fine one at that!"

Thus it was that they decided to pay a visit to the Museum of the History of Science in Piazza dei Giudici. On the first floor, Philip admired their large collection of astrolabes.

"Sailors used these instruments to calculate their course, measuring the distance of the stars from the horizon. In fact, the Greek word for astrolabe means 'starcatcher.' With a tool like this, Columbus would have reached the Indies—if America didn't get in his way, that is. And here's the famous armillary sphere, built at the end of the 1500s."

"How does it work?"

"It's a sphere surrounded by a series of rings that the ancients called *armillae*. The rings are interlocking, and they represent the celestial circles that move around the Earth. It's an old theory, and we'll get to it in a moment. The *armillae* show the move-

ments of the skies, planets and stars—a motion that was reproduced by working the levers."

JUSTUS SUSTERMANS, "PORTRAIT OF GALILEO GALILEI"

GALILEO

"This other section is dedicated to the telescopes of Galileo, the great scientist, philosopher, astronomer, mathematician…"

"Is that all?"

"It will do. Thanks to these telescopes, Galileo was able to disprove Ptolemy by demonstrating that the Earth orbits around the Sun, and not, as it was generally believed, the other way around."

"So tell me a little something about Galileo."

"He went into medicine when he entered university, but fell in love with math and philosophy soon thereafter. That was back in the days when the study of philosophy was essentially the study of Aristotle."

"The great Roman philosopher!"

"*Greek*, Philip, Greek! His theories had an incredible influence over later thought, to the point that for more than 1,500 years, no one even dreamt of contradicting him."

"Now *that* is something I would enjoy."

"Anyway, Galileo got fed up with university life after a while, and started giving private math lessons. In the meantime, he invented a scale with a water mechanism that was so sensitive you could weigh feathers on it. He was a genius… but at first they didn't quite understand him. You see, he applied for the chair of mathematics at the University of Bologna, but didn't get the job. In compensation, the Florentine Academy asked him to lecture on Dante."

THE GREEK PHILOSOPHER ARISTOTLE WITH A PUPIL…

137

"But what did Dante have to do with anything? He was a poet, wasn't he?"

"Of course he was, but in his *Divine Comedy* he described the entire universe, from Hell on up. Galileo was supposed to comment on Dante's conception of the cosmos. Anyway, he eventually won a teaching position in Pisa and, in the meantime, continued his experiments."

"What kind of experiments?"

"For example, he would climb to the top of the Leaning Tower and throw down objects of unequal weights."

"A pastime much like any other."

"That's how he was able to show that the speed of fall of a heavy object is not proportional to its weight, as Aristotle had claimed. But Galileo's colleagues didn't like him contradicting Aristotle and his contract was not renewed… That's when he moved to Padua."

"Didn't he have a private life? I mean, between one experiment and another…"

"Marriage was probably the last thing on his mind: he didn't have much money and he had his own family to maintain. Nevertheless, at a certain point he met a nice Venetian lady, and they had three kids: two girls and a boy."

"That poor little boy, what with two sisters and Galileo breathing down his neck!"

"Galileo didn't give much thought to anything but his studies. He discovered that the distance an object falls is proportional to the square of the time it takes to fall. He also proved that the trajectory of a projectile is always a parabola. Needless to say, both of these conclusions…"

"…contradicted Aristotle."

PLANETS & POLEMICS

"Now here comes the good part. In the spring of 1609, word arrived from the Netherlands that a new invention would permit you to see things happening far away just as though they were nearby."

"I didn't know television had been around that long."

"Don't be silly: I'm talking about the telescope! Galileo learned to build them by himself, and he turned out one after the other, more and more powerful. That same autumn, he looked into the heavens with instruments that magnified up to twenty times! He watched the phases of the Moon, and discovered that its surface was not smooth as was formerly thought, but covered with craters and mountains. He also discovered that Jupiter has four moons, and that with the telescope you can see many more stars than appear to the naked eye. Delighted with his discoveries, he wrote a book about them and dedicated it to Grand Duke Cosimo II de' Medici, whom he had tutored in math during the summer. He baptized the satellites of Jupiter the 'Medicean Planets' in honour of the Medici family."

"Brown-nose!"

"The Grand Duke offered him a post at court, and Galileo returned to Florence. That's where he discovered that Venus goes through phases just like the Moon does."

"Or everybody else, for that matter. What then?"

"In those days, they thought that the sky, stars and planets were perfect and unchanging: the pockmarked surface of the moon proved that this wasn't the case. Moreover, they believed that all celestial bodies orbited around the Earth, and that was refuted by the satellites of Jupiter."

"That obviously orbit around Jupiter."

"And the phases of Venus demonstrate that Venus and Mercury orbit around the Sun. Copernicus had been right all along: all the planets, including the Earth, orbit around the Sun. So the Ptolemaic theory was disproven."

"Hang on a minute…"

"OK. Ptolemy was one of the greatest astronomers of antiquity. The theory that takes his name claims that the Earth is at the centre of the universe and everything else orbits around it. It was considered an unquestionable truth until the end of the

19TH CENTURY COPERNICAN 'PLANETARIUM.' MERCURY, VENUS AND EARTH (WITH THE MOON NEARBY) REVOLVE AROUND THE SUN

KLAUDIOS PTOLEMAIOS, GREEK ASTRONOMER AND MATHEMATICIAN, LIVED AT ALEXANDRIA IN EGYPT IN THE 2ND CENTURY A.D. HIS WORK "MATHEMATICAL COLLECTION" WAS KNOWN AS MEGHÌSTE, 'THE GREATEST'. THE ARAB ASTRONOMERS, WHO STUDIED IT DEEPLY, ADDED THE DEFINITE ARTICLE (AL-MEGHÌSTE) TO GIVE US THE NAME BY WHICH IT IS STILL KNOWN TODAY, THE "ALMAGEST."

NIKOLAJ KOPERNIK (1473-1543), POLISH ASTRONOMER. HIS THEORIES, EXPOUNDED IN HIS "DE REVOLUTIONIBUS ORBIUM COELESTIUM," GREATLY INFLUENCED IMPORTANT FIGURES SUCH AS GALILEO, DESCARTES AND NEWTON.

1500s. That's when a Polish astronomer by the name of Copernicus came into the picture. He offered the hypothesis that it was the Earth which rotated, not only around the sun, but also around its own axis. His theory—also known as 'heliocentric' from *hèlios*, the Greek word for sun—has yet to be disproven."

"Fine. And Galileo?"

"He got into a sparring match over sunspots with a German Jesuit. The Jesuit maintained that these spots were actually small satellites of the Sun, but Galileo proved him wrong, telescope in hand. This created a bit of a problem. All of Galileo's findings seemed to support Copernicus, but the idea that the Earth orbited around the Sun didn't really square with certain passages from the Bible that suggest that it's the Sun that does the moving."

"What if they read the Bible differently in light of these new discoveries?"

"Easier said than done! The Bible wasn't supposed to be interpreted by the first Joe to come along. It was a job reserved for theologians."

"Why?"

"It was a very thorny issue, and the Catholics and Protestants never agreed on it. Galileo confronted the problem in a letter to one of his students, but unfortunately it wound up in the hands of his enemies. They sent a revised and corrected copy straight to the Inquisition."

"Uh-oh."

"While he was in Rome defending himself from the accusations, the Inquisition pronounced the Copernican theory heretical, and banned lots of books.

Though Galileo's name didn't appear in the decree, a cardinal wrote him a threatening letter forbidding him from supporting or defending the Copernican theory."

"One more foul and you're out."

"More or less. But how could you stop someone like Galileo? In fact, not long thereafter he got into a discussion on comets with another Jesuit priest, and wrote another book about it."

"Here we go again."

"It's a work of genius, and very funny too. He called it *Il Saggiatore*, or 'The Assayer.' In it, he describes the foundations of the new scientific method. The funny thing is that the Jesuit was right about the comets! Here, listen to what Galileo had to say: *Philosophy is written in this grand book—I mean the universe—which stands continually open to our gaze. But the book cannot be understood unless one first learns to comprehend the language and read the letters in which it is composed. It is written in the language of mathematics, and its characters are triangles, circles, and other geometric figures, without which it is humanly impossible to understand a single word of it—without them, it is like wandering in vain through a dark labyrinth."*

"And how were these words received?"

AN ARMILLARY SPHERE OF BRASS AND CRYSTAL BY GIROLAMO DELLA VOLPAIA. THE SPHERE ENCLOSED WITHIN THE ARMATURE DEPICTS THE EQUATOR, THE TROPICS, THE ARCTIC AND ANTARCTIC CIRCLES, FOUR MERIDIANS AND THE GREAT BAND OF THE ZODIAC WITH ITS TWELVE SIGNS (IN THE FOREGROUND, CAPRICORN AND AQUARIUS).

SUNDIAL DEDICATED TO GRAND DUKE FRANCESCO, WITH TWO DIFFERENT GNOMONS TO USE AT DIFFERENT TIMES OF DAY.

MEDICI COAT OF ARMS!

"Just when *The Assayer* was due to come out, Cardinal Barberini was elected pope. He was a long-time admirer and patron of Galileo. Galileo dedicated the book to him, and rushed to Rome to discuss his theory of tides, yet another proof of the movement of the Earth."

THE "DIALOGUE" & THE TRIAL

"The pope gave him permission to write a book on his theories of the universe, but warned him to treat the Copernican theory as a simple hypothesis. The *Dialogue Concerning the Two Chief World Systems, Ptolemaic and Copernican* came out in Florence in 1632, with a preface specifying that the ideas expressed therein were purely hypothetical."

"Following all the rules."

"Instead Galileo had his own agenda. In the *Dialogue* there are three characters who discuss the theories among themselves. Salviati is Galileo's spokesman, and is, naturally, Copernican. Sagredo is the no-nonsense guy who admits 'I really don't understand any of this stuff,' but who just happens to agree with everything Salviati has to say. Finally, there's Simplicio, the dyed-in-the-wool Aristotelian."

"Simplicio—simpleton" Philip translated, snickering. "That's a low blow."

"That's nothing. Galileo starts with an overview of the arguments supporting the Copernican theory. Then he gives the last work to Simplicio, who serves as a mouthpiece for the pope's favourite theory—that God could make the universe *appear* to us in one way while having created it in another."

"Seems fair enough."

"Formally speaking, perhaps. But Simplicio is the nitwit of the story from start to finish—Galileo never misses an opportunity to put him down. So you see that even if what he says at the end makes sense…"

"…no one was ever going to take it seriously."

"The pope set up a special commission to examine the book: they picked up on Galileo's real intent right away, and gave their go-ahead to the Inquisition."

"Yikes!"

"The Inquisition summoned him to Rome, and slapped down the

edict forbidding him to discuss the Copernican theory. Galileo retorted that he had been forbidden to *defend* the theory, not to *discuss* it. To cut a long story short, he was suspected of heresy, condemned to life imprisonment and forced to abjure formally."

"Abjure?"

"Recant his statements in public. But while he was abjuring, he apparently muttered 'And yet it moves'—referring to the Earth, of course."

"What a nightmare."

"It must have been pretty rough. At least they didn't torture him. He was confined to his villa in Arcetri, near Florence, where he stayed practically under house arrest for the remainder of his life."

"So what did he do?"

"He secretly continued his research. His house was located in a favourable position on top of a hill. It's not by chance that today there's an astronomical observatory not far from his home. He wrote another book that was smuggled out of Italy and then published in the Netherlands. He had gone blind in the meantime, and worked with the help of a young student."

'Sad story...' Philip thought. He could almost picture the great old scientist shut up in his house with his burned-out eyes, eyes that had boldly seen what no one had ever seen before...

"I think I'll send dad a postcard of the telescope."

"And the armillary sphere?"

"It's out of style. We have to stay up-to-date."

Back in the hotel, Philip took out the postcard destined for his parents. He thought of all the family arguments and debates where he had unjustly wound up on the losing side, and wrote *When you're right, you're right. And love to you all.*

A DETAIL OF THE "ADORATION OF THE MAGI" (OR PORTINARI TRIPTYCH, NAMED AFTER ITS PATRON, TOMMASO PORTINARI) BY HUGO VAN DER GOES

THE UFFIZI

HISTORY OF THE MUSEUM

T he time has come. May the Force be with you, young Skywalker."

"The time to do what, exactly?"

"To visit the Uffizi! Now that you've got a sense of the principal styles and most important painters, you're ready to confront a couple hundred masterpieces… and, of course, some of the most charming women in the history of western art!"

"For example?"

"For example, the Madonnas of Filippo Lippi and Botticelli."

"And that naked lady on the shell?"

"Yep, she's there too. The Uffizi… how can I put it?"

"Even I've heard the name before, so it must be one of those museums with a capital M."

SANDRO BOTTICELLI, "MADONNA OF THE MAGNIFICAT"

"To say the least. The Uffizi houses one of the most incredible collections in the world. Very few museums can hold a candle to it: the Louvre in Paris, the National Gallery in London, the Prado in Madrid… Plus, there's the charm of the building itself: it looks like a theatre backdrop wedged between Palazzo Vecchio and the Arno. It was built for Cosimo I by his trusty architect Giorgio Vasari, and originally served as the offices—or *uffici*—of the Grand Duchy."

"So that's why it's called the Uffizi!"

"Exactly. Then, Cosimo's son Francesco —the Studiolo guy—transformed the top floor into a splendid gallery for some of his antique statues and a number of works of art from his collection. Thus was born the first museum in the world. There was also a theatre inside, where they put on plays with sumptuous sets and elaborate, sometimes bizarre stage machinery. There were even shops where they sold luxury items, perfumes and sweets."

"Interesting…"

A stone staircase led them up to a long corridor.

"Here we are, in the famous gallery. It's still got various ancient statues on display, and this wonderful ceiling decorated with grotesques. We'd better keep moving…"

Filippo Lippi, "Madonna & Child with Angels"

FILIPPO LIPPI HAD A RATHER ADVENTUROUS LIFE. BOTH HIS PARENTS DIED WHILE HE WAS STILL VERY YOUNG. HE LIVED WITH AN AUNT FOR A WHILE, THEN IN 1421 HE TOOK CARMELITE VOWS AND ENTERED THE FRIARY OF SANTA MARIA DEL CARMINE. JUST AT THAT TIME MASACCIO AND MASOLINO WERE PAINTING THE FRESCOES IN THE BRANCACCI CHAPEL: THE YOUNG FRIAR WAS ENCHANTED, AND DECIDED THAT HE TOO WOULD BECOME A PAINTER. IT WAS AT THIS POINT, IF WE CAN BELIEVE VASARI, THAT DISASTER STRUCK: FILIPPO WAS SAILING WITH SOME FRIENDS IN THE ADRIATIC WHEN HE WAS KIDNAPPED BY PIRATES! IMPRISONED AND SOLD INTO SLAVERY, FILIPPO WAS DETAINED FOR A YEAR AND A HALF: HIS OWNER ONLY RELEASED HIM AFTER FILIPPO HAD PAINTED HIS PORTRAIT. BACK IN FLORENCE, HE BEGAN TO RECEIVE MANY COMMISSIONS FOR PAINTINGS IN CHURCHES AND CONVENTS FROM THE MEDICI FAMILY. BUT STILL HE DID NOT HAVE A QUIET LIFE, APPARENTLY BECAUSE HE WAS EXCEEDINGLY FOND OF WOMEN… IN 1456, WHILE HE WAS PAINTING FRESCOES IN THE CONVENT OF SANTA MARGHERITA IN PRATO, HE FELL IN LOVE WITH A YOUNG NUN CALLED LUCREZIA, AND PERSUADED HER TO RUN AWAY WITH HIM. THEIR ELOPEMENT CAUSED QUITE A SCANDAL, BUT THE POPE HIMSELF DECIDED TO ALLOW THEM TO GET MARRIED: THEY SOON HAD A BABY, FILIPPINO, WHO ALSO BECAME A FAMOUS PAINTER. THE LITTLE FAMILY WENT TO LIVE IN PRATO. FILIPPO IS HOWEVER BURIED IN SPOLETO, WHERE HE HAD GONE TO DECORATE THE CHOIR OF THE CATHEDRAL TOGETHER WITH HIS FAITHFUL ASSISTANT FRA DIAMANTE.

14TH-CENTURY MADONNAS

There were three large Madonnas on huge gilded panels waiting for them in the first room.

"They might look similar at first glance: they're all enthroned, which is why they're called *Maestà*, or 'Majesties.' They all hold the Child in their arms, and are surrounded by angels or saints. They were all painted during the same years—more or less. But the very fact that they share the same subject highlights the differences among them. This one in the middle is by Giotto. What does our critic have to say about it?"

"Compared to the other two… she looks a little more comfortable. The throne is deeper and roomier."

"Because Giotto was more concerned with anatomy and space. The *chiaroscuro* technique brings out the chest and knees, drawing them out. Aside from the blessing

145

New!

Cimabue

"Santa Trinita Madonna"

Duccio

"Rucellai Madonna"

Giotto

"Ognissanti Madonna"

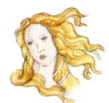

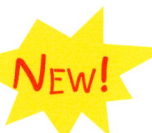

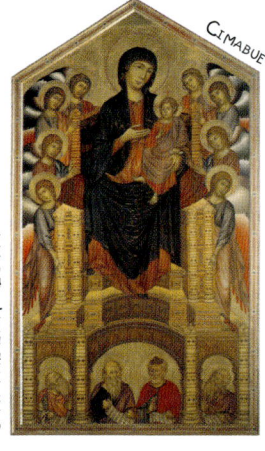

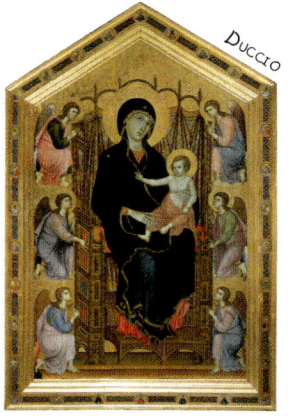

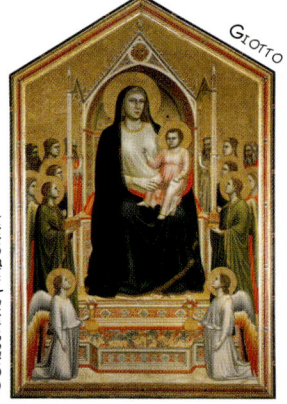

he gives with his little hand, Jesus looks a baby in flesh and blood. Cimabue's stylized *Maestà* is clearly the most similar to the figures we saw in the baptistery; whereas the Sienese artist Duccio gets points for his colours and draperies. Go behind the Giotto for a minute, and see how a panel from the 1300s was made."

The next room was dedicated to Sienese artists from the 1300s. Philip was fascinated by Simone Martini's *Annunciation*.

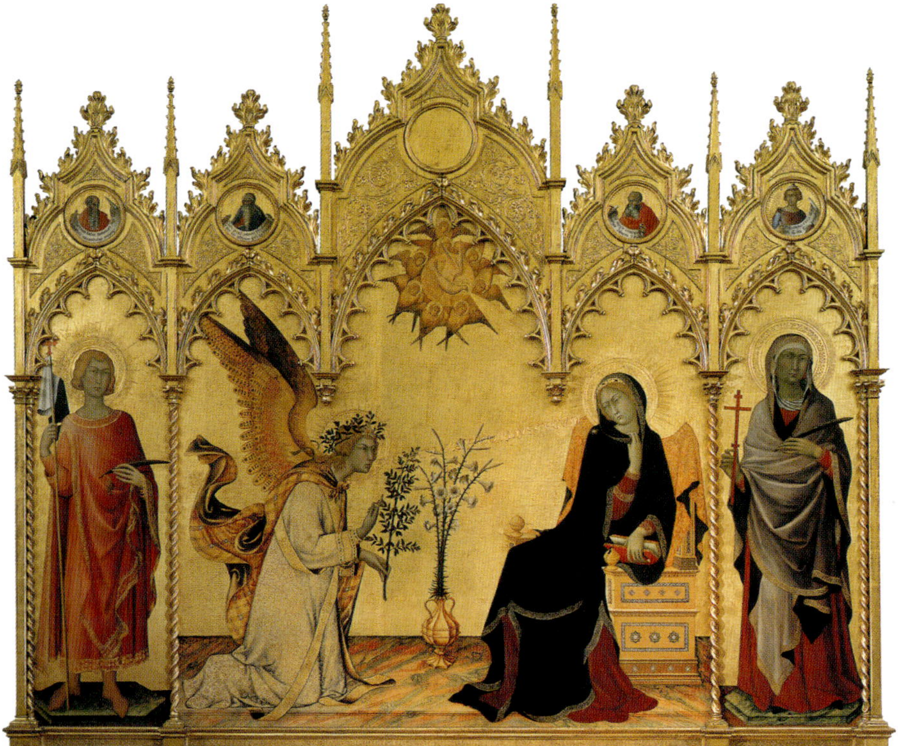

Clear, cool & sweet waters, where she who alone seems to me a true lady refreshed her lovely limbs...

"Siena was Florence's rival in Tuscany, a rich and sophisticated city with a fascinating history of her own... We'll save that for some other time. This is a truly exceptional piece: the precious fabrics, the gold work, the pale and elegant figures... With his delicate brushstroke, Simone managed to create not only a mystic, surreal atmosphere, but also one full of details. 19th-century aesthetes were crazy about this piece: which is not surprising, given their penchant for Persian miniatures and Japanese prints. Ah yes, Simone was one high-class painter. Not many people know that he and his family eventually moved to Avignon, France, where he met the great poet Francesco Petrarca—Petrarch, that is. They lived in the same neighbourhood and became good friends. Petrarch had a codex of the works of Virgil, and Simone painted a miniature on the cover for him. He also did a portrait of the famous Laura—the woman Petrarch was madly in love with, and his inspiration for countless poems."

"What was she like?"

"According to Petrarch, she was gorgeous. Unfortunately the portrait was lost; we'll have to take his word for it."

147

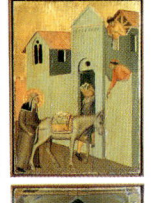

"And what's this painting here? It looks very much like a comic strip."

"That's the *Altarpiece of the Blessed Umiltà* by Pietro Lorenzetti. It illustrates the life of nuns in a convent. The little figure at the foot of the Saint is the nun who commissioned the painting: she specifically requested to be painted so small."

"Speaking of humility…"

"It didn't last for long: over time, clients left modesty to the wayside. You'll get the idea when we go into the room of 14th-century Florentine Art. There are two women in Giottino's *Pietà*: a nun and a rich young lady with a precious waistband. Though they're still smaller than the sacred figures, they're already up to the shoulders of the saints surrounding the body of Jesus!"

148

GENTILE DA FABRIANO

A few minutes later, the two found themselves in the room of International Gothic, admiring the *Adoration of the Magi* by Gentile da Fabriano.

"I love International Gothic," Uncle Charlie declared. "It's an elegant, refined style that spread through European courts in the 1300s and 1400s." He added: "The painting that you have before you is a true masterpiece. It was commissioned by Palla Strozzi for his family chapel in Santa Trinita."

"He must have spent a small fortune."

"You bet. Gentile da Fabriano was a respected artist, and his work was expensive. Anyway, Palla had money coming out his ears: he was the richest man in Florence and when he wanted something, he got it. He wanted this altarpiece to be the most fabulous anyone had ever seen—does that sound familiar? So he called in the best guy in town to do it."

"That is, Gentile."

"Exactly. He was born in Fabriano, but he travelled quite a bit: Orvieto, Venice, Brescia, Florence and Rome, where he died. Unfortunately, many of his most important works have been lost: a fire here, vandalism there. Anyway, he arrived in Florence in 1422, got himself a house in the Santa Trinita neighbourhood, enrolled with the Physicians' and Apothecaries' Guild and got to work. The following year, the painting was finished. Even Michelangelo, despite his very different style of painting, held him in the highest regard. He said that in painting Gentile's hand was similar to his name, which in Italian means kind and gentle." Uncle Charlie was enjoying himself. "*La mano simile al nome.* That's clever, isn't it?"

"So let's take a look at this masterpiece, shall we?"

"We'll start from the top. The *tondi* set in the spires—from left to right—represent the Angel of the Annunciation, the Judging Christ, and the Virgin Annunciate. The main story begins at top left, where the Three Kings behold the star. Then they're depicted on the road to Bethlehem. To the top right, you see them in front of the city gates. Finally, in the foreground, the kings are shown at the manger."

"The star grows brighter the closer they get."

"That's right. Gentile had a weakness for light effects: he was ahead of his time as far as that goes."

ELEGANT FLORAL DECORATION (FROM THE CLOTHING OF THE YOUNGEST KING IN THE FOREGROUND)

"But what do all those people have to do with the Adoration?"

"Absolutely nothing! But you see, this is more than just a religious painting. It's… how can I put it? A voyage of knights, an elaborate fairy tale. You wanted lambs and shepherds like your run-of-the-mill crèche? Not on your life! I'm going to paint you a cortège from the late Middle Ages: a smart company of noblemen returning from the hunt and paying homage to an aristocratic damsel. In the meantime, look: there's practically no spatial relationship between the scene in the foreground and the one in the back."

"What's that supposed to mean?"

"It means that there's no 'front' and 'behind,' but only an 'upper' and 'lower.' That's important, because it reflects an underlying choice."

"Let's have it."

"Gentile wasn't particularly interested in space and volume. He was attracted to the *surface* of things, and loved to reproduce it in meticulous detail. How can

I explain this? It's like he was more interested in the fuzzy skin of a peach than he was in the fruit itself. If you look closely, you'll see that every figure seems to have been studied under a microscope and broken down into a million details: the sumptuous, velvety fabrics, the precious ornamentation... And take a look at this stuff! Scattered among the suitors you find monkeys, greyhounds, falcons, camels, cheetahs and more... Gentile was blessed with a unique curiosity and an exquisite taste for detail."

"Peach-fuzz fascination... I'm going to write that one down."

"But wait, there's more! The pilasters have become hollow, fretworked Gothic spires. Instead of the usual saints, the spires host plants of every kind: clover, violets, lilies, brooms, chickpeas, poppies, jasmines... I don't know what that one is... gentians, strawberries, cherries, daisies, carnations, et cetera. He was one of the first to dabble in still life! And look: the gold was actually embossed at certain points: the belts, the bridles, spurs, sword hilts, dog collars... And don't forget that having these rich fabrics actually painted was a great form of advertising: in those days, Florentine weavers were coming out with some incredibly luxurious articles."

"I won't. Mostly I won't forget that you're crazy about this painting."

"I sure am. Because you see, it's really the portrait of an epoch: of that elegant and refined era that is sometimes called the Autumn of the Middle Ages. Here's our friend Palla staring back at us. He wasn't about to be a little background figure: he's there at the centre of the painting with the dark red turban and the black outfit edged in gold."

"He almost seems to be saying 'take a good look, kids. I *paid* for this puppy!'"

"You'll have to admit... it was money well-spent."

Masaccio & Paolo Uccello

"And now," Uncle Charlie solemnly announced, "welcome to the Renaissance. These rooms display the most famous works of the new style that was 'invented,' as we surely recall, by..."

"Brunelleschi, Donatello and Masaccio!"

"Very good. Brunelleschi had rediscovered perspective, and Donatello had studied anatomy so well that he was able to express gestures and emotions with startling realism. Masaccio owed a lot to both of them, incorporating their innovations into his painting. He and Masolino painted this *Madonna and St Anne*. Masolino was still tied to the Gothic style, whereas Masaccio, as we saw in Santa Maria Novella, was a good Renaissance man. He carefully arranged his objects in

IT WAS THE FAMOUS ART HISTORIAN AND CRITIC ROBERTO LONGHI WHO ATTRIBUTED THE UPPER PORTION OF THIS PICTURE TO MASOLINO AND THE LOWER PORTION TO MASACCIO

MASOLINO

MASACCIO

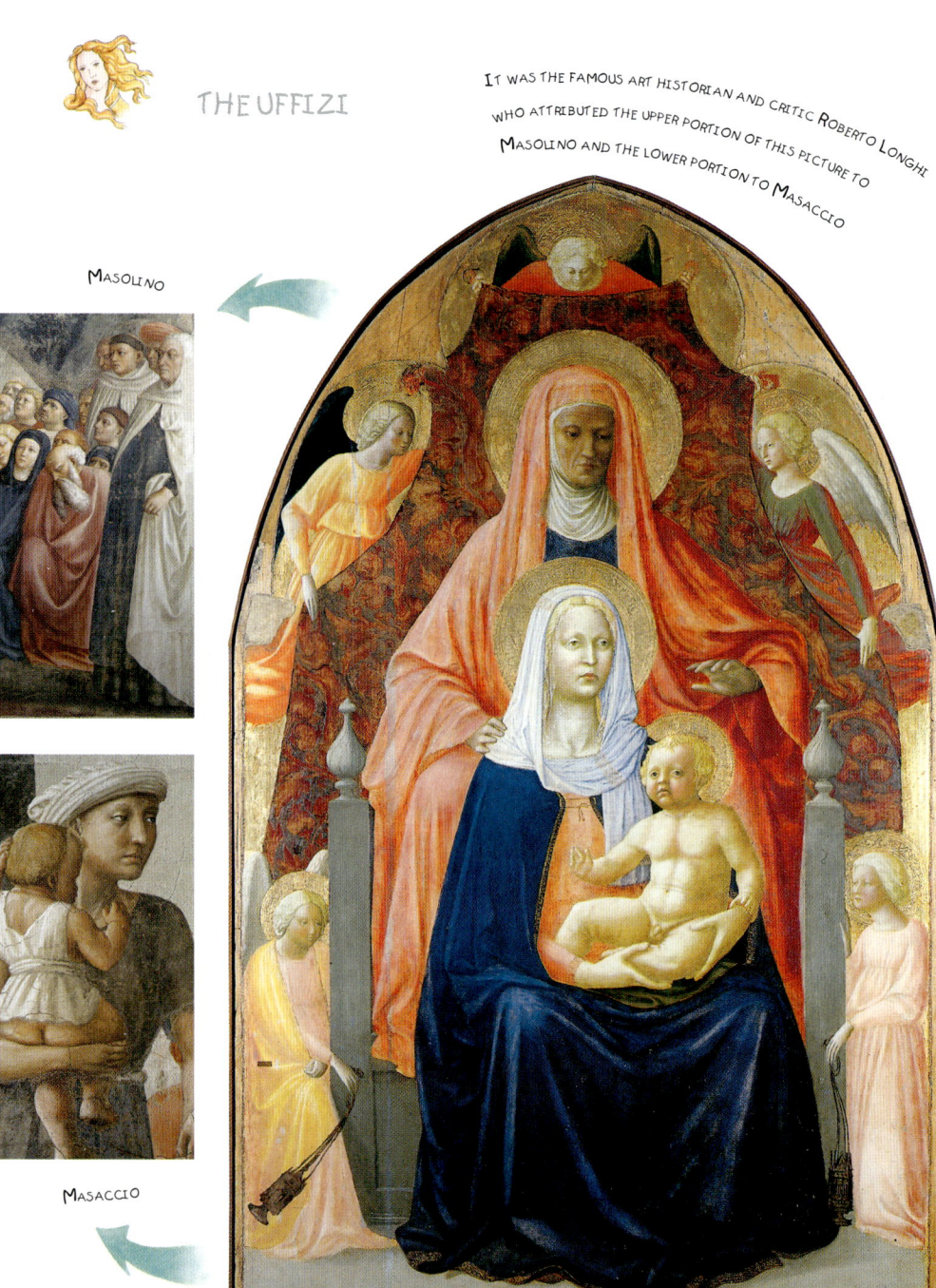

space, and used colour not only to decorate, but also to give his figures a certain depth and solidity, the illusion of volume. So now the big question is: who painted what?"

"What do I win if I guess it right?"

"Knowledge is a reward unto itself."

"Very funny. So… The body of the Madonna seems more studied to me, and fits better into space… The Child too, who stands on her lap. I don't know about St Anne… she looks flatter somehow, both her body and her face. It looks like she's wearing a sort of mask, and like she's behind the other figures. I mean, she *is*, but…"

"You're right! The Virgin and Child were painted by Masaccio, while Masolino worked on St Anne and the angels."

"Yeah, the angels, too… with their hands looking a little… dislocated."

"Don't get me wrong: Masolino was hardly a second-rate painter. It's just that the new Renaissance style was not exactly his cup of tea."

"But this Masaccio who was so far ahead of his time, did he just pop out of nowhere?"

"More or less. His real name was Tommaso di Giovanni di Simone Cassai, but everyone called him Masaccio. He was the only artist in his family: his father was a notary and his mom was the daughter of an innkeeper. But his father's father built wooden chests that were then painted with decorations: perhaps he watched them done as a boy and decided to become a painter. The problem is that no one knows where, when or with whom he studied."

"What do you mean?"

"In those days, if you wanted to become an artist, you had to become the apprentice of an established painter or sculptor. It took years and years to move up through the ranks of the workshop. Once you learned the tricks of the trade, you could set up a *bottega* of your own. Naturally, the young apprentices imitated the style of their own *maestro*. Unfortunately, we know nothing about Masaccio until the time he enrolled in the Physicians' and Apothecaries' Guild… and therefore, nothing about who influenced him."

"Which would be a clue as to why his painting was so innovative."

"Precisely. And who knows what he might have accomplished had he lived a longer life: he didn't even reach his twenty-seventh birthday."

"You're kidding!"

"I know, it's incredible—especially considering the influence he had… He was like a Mozart of the painting world."

"Whoa now. Who did this… *thing*?"

"I thought you'd like it. Who else but Paolo Uccello, the Duo-

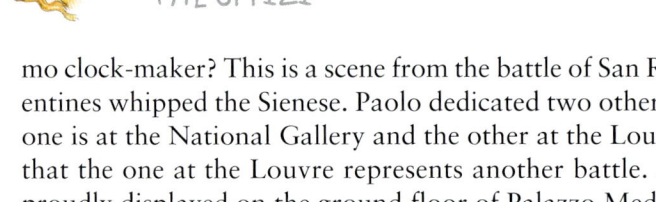

mo clock-maker? This is a scene from the battle of San Romano, where the Flor-entines whipped the Sienese. Paolo dedicated two other paintings to this battle: one is at the National Gallery and the other at the Louvre—even if some claim that the one at the Louvre represents another battle. Anyway, all three were proudly displayed on the ground floor of Palazzo Medici. They were probably commissioned by Cosimo the Elder, who was a good friend of the mercenary captain that led the Florentine troops, Niccolò da Tolentino. The paintings were originally in the shape of lunettes, and were only later cut into rectangles. What do you say?"

"I'd say it's a pretty weird-looking battle scene. For one thing, it isn't particu-larly bloody. For another, it's almost like… a video on pause, or like a shot in slow motion. I can almost buy the green and orange horses, but the warriors… they don't even look like men in that smooth, jointed armour. They look like the bad guys in *Star Wars*!"

"Vasari himself was perplexed by the colours. He said that Paolo painted *blue fields, red cities, and the buildings in whatever colours suited him.* As for the rest, you pretty much quoted a great art critic, even if he probably never saw *Star Wars*. The painting's not so much a human battle scene as it is a clash between geometric shapes and foreshortened perspective. The palisade of spears, stand-ards, coats of arms—it all hearkens back to an age gone by, conjuring images of jousts and medieval knights. Note that the distribution of full and empty spaces is refined and experimental."

"And the armour?"

"It was covered with gold and silver leaf, and sparkled like the real thing. Paolo used very expensive lacquers and resins here (including a precious one known as 'dragon's blood'), and no one had ever seen this kind of extravagance in Floren-tine art. It was part of the Gothic legacy, but Ghiberti's influence played into it, as did Paolo's stay in Venice. Once again, Paolo arranged the space in his own unique way: rigorous, motionless, abstract. He used perspective to help ground the figures, but he made up his own rules as far as their dimensions were con-cerned. Look at the background: spears that poke up from the hills, soldiers in the hedges, people with crossbows and frightened animals running for their lives."

"And a rabbit jumping over a pine tree!"

"That's just my point. Paolo Uccello was a singular fellow. In Gothic art he loved the details and vibrant colours, its linear, decorative style. But he also admired the solemnity of Donatello's and Masaccio's art, their realism, and the clarity of their perspective. So what did he do?"

"What?"

"He experimented. He took the new, true-to-life figures and simplified them into abstract geometric forms. He took perspective and explored its most extreme and bizarre qualities. He remained, however, forever drawn to the old Gothic world, the magic world of fairy tales. That's why there are so many opposites in

LONDON

FLORENCE

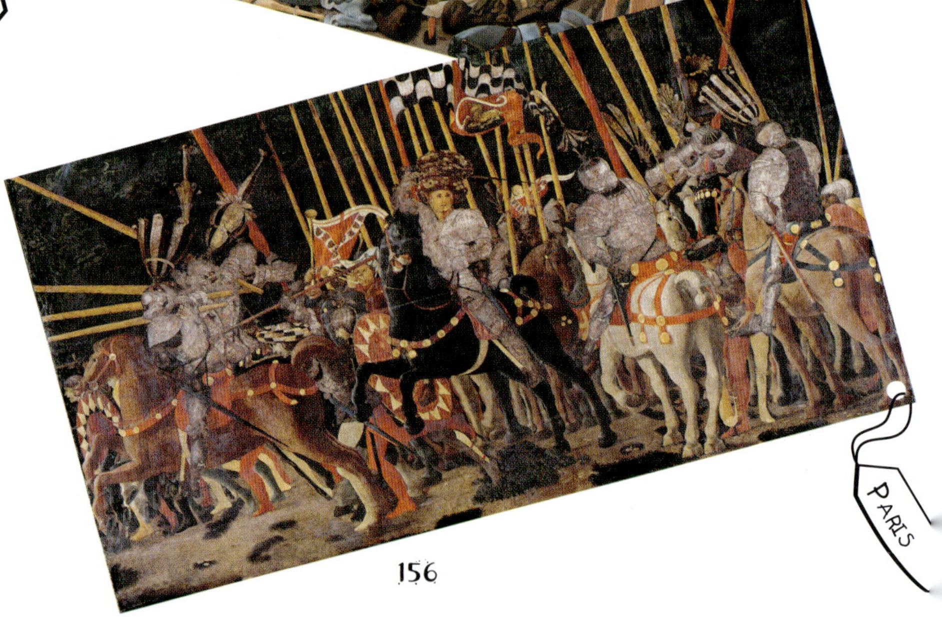

PARIS

his work: the clear and the muddled, the simple and complex, calculation and imagination... Each and every one of his paintings holds some innovation and surprise in store. And he never gave up his ironic and whimsical style."

"THE BIRTH OF VENUS" & "PRIMAVERA"

"Behold Botticelli!" Uncle Charlie boomed, badly startling a couple of elderly German tourists. One of them had dropped her sunglasses in alarm, and the archaeologist hurried to retrieve them with an embarrassed grin. The woman rewarded him with an acid remark about 'the young people of today,' but he didn't quite catch it.

"This is where things get a little tricky. These paintings were done for the Medici family, who were a pretty sophisticated lot. The mythological subjects of his most famous works, including the *Birth of Venus* and *Primavera*, are actually very intricate allegories. Mysterious characters are found alongside divinities of the classical world, and only after long years of research were the scholars able to make sense of them."

"I, on the other hand, after a long minute of reflection, haven't understood a single thing."

"I'll give you an example. Take this panel with *Minerva Restraining the Centaur*. Minerva—or Athena, the goddess of wisdom—holds a centaur by the hair. This centaur, a creature half-man and half-horse, represents instinct.

So, the scene is supposed to illus-trate that wisdom is able to restrain instinct, and the two figures would thus be personified concepts. But there's yet another level of symbol-ism. Note that Minerva is wearing a white robe embroidered with the famous Medici rings."

"The ones we saw at the chapel."

"Right. Also, she's crowned with laurel—the Magnificent's favourite plant and his emblem of choice."

"So she represents the Medici?"

"Yes. The painting basically says that Lorenzo was able to check the brutality of war with diplomacy. Piece of cake, right?"

"You bet. So who did this know-it-all think he was, anyway?"

"Botticelli was the son of a leather

tanner, but he had an education. At a certain point he decided to become a painter, and apprenticed with Filippo Lippi."

"The one who did the Madonna we saw earlier."

"Yes, a great artist who had a lot of influence over Botticelli's style. Botticelli was then welcomed into the Medici circle, frequented by poets and philosophers, and he became their favourite painter. Wait, I almost forgot: after the Pazzi Conspiracy, they had him paint portraits of all of the people hanged at the Bargello."

"What an honour!"

"Sometimes one had to accept a little dirty work… Anyway, he was extremely popular for a while, and the last decades of the century were his moment in the sun. Then he went into a downslide."

"How come?"

"Lorenzo had passed away and the political climate wasn't the healthiest… And then there was Girolamo Savonarola, the Dominican friar, thundering from the pulpit against society's corrupted ways. Botticelli started cleaning up his act, as many of his paintings had fairly daring themes for the time. Then Savonarola was condemned and burned at the stake for heresy. Botticelli couldn't make heads or tails of it, and went into a full-blown spiritual crisis. The world that he had loved, and that had honoured him, didn't exist anymore. He decided to stick with

religious themes and moralistic allegories. In the meantime—we're talking about the early 1500s—a new generation of top-rate artists was emerging: Leonardo da Vinci, Raphael, Michelangelo… Poor old Botticelli was soon overshadowed, and he won fewer and fewer jobs. By the time he died, people had already forgotten about him."

"But he's totally famous today!"

"It's hard to believe, but for centuries he remained a famous unknown. He was rediscovered in the 1800s by the English: art historians like Ruskin and Pater, and most of all the Pre-Raphaelites, artists who loved pre-1500s Italian art and used it as a model and an inspiration for their own works. From then on, Botticelli grew more famous with every passing day. Let's take a look at his work. This is the 'Woman on the Shell,' more commonly known as the *Birth of Venus*. At the centre, the goddess of beauty rises from the sea atop a gigantic shell. The winds of the sky swirl upon her, and the young and lovely Hora—the spirit of seasons— is poised on the coast, ready to cover her with a flowered cloak. The colours are tenuous, almost transparent, and there are no strong shadows, only vibrations of light on the pale skin and the creases of the clothing…"

"Where there is any clothing at all."

"Right. The composition is symmetrical and balanced. It's a celebration of beauty at its most natural, simple and pure."

Philip snickered and his uncle beat him to the punch: "I know, it sounds like an ad for mineral water. But what did you expect: I mean, I never pretended to be an art historian."

"You're doing great. Go ahead."

THE "PRIMAVERA" WAS COMMISSIONED FROM SANDRO BOTTICELLI BY LORENZO DE' MEDICI: NOT THE MAGNIFICENT, BUT HIS SECOND COUSIN, KNOWN AS 'THE COMMONER,' SON OF PIERFRANCESCO AND GRANDSON OF LORENZO THE ELDER, WHO WAS THE BROTHER OF COSIMO THE ELDER, GRANDFATHER OF LORENZO THE MAGNIFICENT. SO THIS WAS A CADET BRANCH OF THE FAMILY, THOUGH NOT FOR LONG: THE SON OF THE BROTHER OF THIS LORENZO WAS NONE OTHER THAN THE GREAT MERCENARY COMMANDER GIOVANNI DALLE BANDE NERE, FATHER OF THE FUTURE GRAND DUKE COSIMO I. IS EVERYTHING CLEAR? NEVER MIND: THIS LONG PREAMBLE WAS JUST TO GET YOU IN THE MOOD TO ENJOY THIS FAMOUS PAINTING, WHICH IN FACT... ACTUALLY, WE'RE NOT SURE WHAT IT REPRESENTS. WE ONLY KNOW THAT BOTTICELLI TOOK HIS INSPIRATION FROM SOME ANCIENT AUTHORS (THE LATIN POETS LUCRETIUS AND OVID, FOR INSTANCE) AND FROM SOME MODERN ONES (THE PHILOSOPHER FICINO AND THE POET POLITIAN). WHAT CAN WE SAY? THE SUBJECT OF THE PAINTING SEEMS TO BE LOVE, IN ITS TWO ASPECTS: THE PHYSICAL AND THE INTELLECTUAL, I.E. THE IMPULSE TOWARDS WHAT IS BEAUTIFUL AND GOOD (NOT GOOD TO EAT, OF COURSE), WHICH RAISES THE SPIRIT OF MANKIND TOWARDS HIGHER THINGS. TO CUT A LONG STORY SHORT, STARTING FROM THE RIGHT WE HAVE THE FOLLOWING: (a) ZEPHYR AND THE NYMPH CHLORIS REPRESENT PHYSICAL LOVE AS THE SOURCE OF LIFE; FROM THEIR UNION IS BORN FLORA, GODDESS OF SPRING; (b) FLORA STREWS THE EARTH WITH FLOWERS AND MAKES IT FERTILE; (c) IN THE CENTRE, THE GODDESS VENUS UNITES AND SEPARATES THE TWO KINDS OF LOVE; (d) UP ABOVE, BLIND CUPID SHOOTS AN ARROW TOWARDS THE THREE GRACES; (e) THE GRACES, SYMBOL OF HARMONY AND OF PURE LOVE, DANCE GRACEFULLY (WHAT DID YOU EXPECT?), BUT (f) ONE OF THEM, CHASTITY, LOOKS LONGINGLY AT MERCURY (WHO REPRESENTS REASON); (g) HE DOES NOT RECIPROCATE, BUT GAZES UPWARDS, DISPELLING THE CLOUDS OF DOUBT, AND LAUNCHING THE LOVE OF MANKIND INTO THE HEAVENLY EMPYREAN.

"Since you're having so much fun at my expense," the archaeologist continued, "we'll move on to something more difficult. The *Primavera* is one of Botticelli's most animated paintings, and has several wonderful characters. What's more, it's like this guy is actually *proposing* to the line. Lines everywhere—our painter interweaves them and dissolves them continuously, giving the composition a delicate, slow and graceful rhythm. The painting is read from right to left. Here, take the guide and read what it has to say about it."

Philip took the book and started reading. It was a hassle, because every three seconds he had to look up from the page to study the painting. After a few minutes he stopped, perplexed. "Here it says that in the end, Mercury sends the clouds away and pushes love towards the heavens."

"And at the beginning, there's Zephyr that descends from the sky… Get it? It's a circle, a continuous, never-ending cycle."

"Clear as crystal," Philip said doubtfully. "Anyway, I don't mind. It's like a brain-teaser just waiting to be solved."

"And the solution—that is, the real subject of the painting—is love in all its nuances, in perfect equilibrium between the physical and spiritual sides. But here's the curious thing: the 'fathers' of the Renaissance had excavated and examined

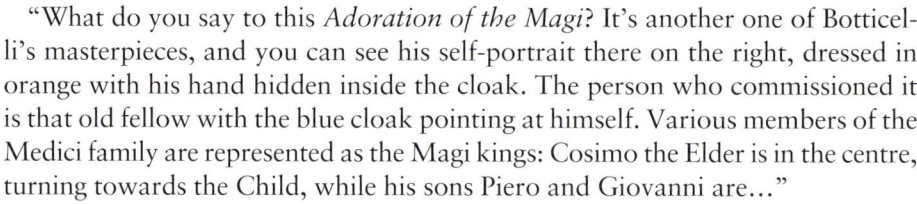

sculptures and monuments from antiquity, deliberately seeking the secret of their harmony. Botticelli, on the other hand, did not. Though he borrowed many myths and symbols from the classical world, he didn't actually *study* the past. He merely looked back on it with nostalgia. A marvellous world, but hopelessly out of reach."

"Hey, listen—how about something simpler for a change? That we can just look at?"

"What do you say to this *Adoration of the Magi*? It's another one of Botticelli's masterpieces, and you can see his self-portrait there on the right, dressed in orange with his hand hidden inside the cloak. The person who commissioned it is that old fellow with the blue cloak pointing at himself. Various members of the Medici family are represented as the Magi kings: Cosimo the Elder is in the centre, turning towards the Child, while his sons Piero and Giovanni are…"

"Not again! Who did they think they were, anyway?"

"And that cocky-looking lad standing to the left is the young Lorenzo, wearing white tights."

![Leonardo da Vinci, Adoration of the Magi]

LEONARDO & MICHELANGELO

"Here's another *Adoration*," Philip observed.

"Yes, this one's by Leonardo da Vinci. Not surprisingly, he has a very original take on the theme. In the centre, the Virgin Mary holds the Child on her lap. The other characters, including the Magi, crowd around them. They're sporting a wonderful variety of expressions, each one masterfully reproduced. They all react to the birth of Jesus in a different way: wonder, admiration, indifference, hope… even fear—look at those spooked horses. Unfortunately, Leonardo had an ugly falling out with the man who ordered the painting, so it was never finished: all we have to go on are the sketch and *chiaroscuro*. Anyway, we can still appreciate the beauty and originality of the work."

"Like Michelangelo's *Prisoners*: those weren't finished either. Look, uncle, this *Annunciation* is by Leonardo, too."

"Good catch. It's no coincidence that the angel's wings look like real bird wings. Leonardo was fascinated by flight and studied its dynamics. He even designed his own wings, helicopters and hang gliders. The scene unfolds on the flowered lawn of a villa. The Angel kneels in front of Mary; and the trees in the background are all different from each other—a real exercise in style… You can make out a misty landscape in the distance, shrouded, so it seems, in fog. What do you say, shall we take a look at one last piece?"

"As long as it's not by Botticelli."

Philip's uncle led him to the third corridor of the gallery, where Michelangelo's *Holy Family* is on display. The work is better known as the Doni Tondo, named after its round shape and the Doni family that commissioned it.

"Michelangelo's artistic ideal was always essentially sculptural and plastic. He meant it when he wrote: *I say that painting is considered well-done the more it resembles relief, whereas relief is considered poorly done the more it resembles a painting*. This one is the only painting on canvas that we know for certain to be his work. Seated next to St Joseph, the Virgin Mary holds the Child almost on her shoulders: a truly original pose. And look at the nudes behind them: they represent mankind before God handed the Commandments down to Moses. Young St John the Baptist peeks up from behind a low wall, serving as a bridge between the Old and New Testaments. Typically for Michelangelo, the figures are nice and full, robust and muscular. They convey a wonderful sense of strength and physical tension."

"Would that be the same kind of tension I'm feeling in my legs?"

"Let's go. You earned yourself a double-decker tripe sandwich!"

AGNOLO BRONZINO PAINTED THIS PORTRAIT
OF BIA, COSIMO I'S ILLEGITIMATE DAUGHTER,
AROUND 1542 (UFFIZI, TRIBUNE).

THE PRINCE'S PASSAGEWAY

TAKE-OFF

fter their intense visit to the Uffizi, Charles decided that they would spend the next day in the hills around Florence: silent back roads, woods, country houses among the vineyards and naturally, as Gabriele D'Annunzio put it, *the brother olives, that pale the hillsides with their sanctity…*

"Listen, Uncle Charlie," Philip began during one of their walks through the countryside, "are there any gardens in Florence other than the one at the Stibbert? I mean, a *real* garden—not just a little square with two trees and a swing set."

"Certainly! There's a splendid garden, and a crowded one at that: you can barely count all the gods, grottoes, fountains and monsters!"

"Where is it?"

"We'll have to cross the Arno. How do we get there: by ground or by air?"

"You mean… in a helicopter?"

"Even better."

Philip was starting to have some serious doubts about his uncle's mental health, but he limited his response to a dry "Given the choice, I'd go by air."

The next morning, the two were back in Palazzo Vecchio's Green Room.

"There's our man," Uncle Charles declared, pointing at a stocky fellow who was approaching with a large bunch of keys. The custodian unlocked a door and gestured for them to follow.

"Where are we going?"

"Our voyage by air has just begun. This catwalk leads to the Uffizi."

ROSSO FIORENTINO, "MUSICIAN ANGEL"

"And the Arno?"

"All things in due time, O nephew of little faith!"

The custodian took his leave, muttering obscure words: "In ten minutes, outside the Room of Michelangelo."

"Good. Now, let's make the most of it and have a look at the Tribune."

Increasingly bewildered, Philip followed his uncle into a lavish octagonal room. The domed roof was faced with mother-of-pearl, the walls with red velvet, and the floors paved with multicoloured semi-precious stone.

"Not bad, huh? This is where the gallery masterpieces used to be displayed. The ebony shelving along the walls was specially designed to hold rare objects: precious stones, medals and small bronze statues. It was known as the 'Room of Wonders,' the heart of the entire gallery."

"I've seen those two before."

"Those are Cosimo I and the duchess Eleonora, wearing her elaborate wedding gown. Their first-born, Francesco, is painted as a boy with a letter in his hand. He's the one who commissioned the Tribune. The design was done by his friend and partner in 'oddities,' Bernardo Buontalenti. The Tribune, as well as being a place of wonders, was built according to a precise symbolic design."

"Meaning?"

"It represents the cosmos with its four basic elements or 'components,' which are, of course, air, water, earth and fire."

"Let me guess: fire is the red of the walls, water is the mother-of-pearl of the dome, earth is the pavement in semi-precious stone, and air…"

"…is that little flag weathervane—by the way, it still works. Come along, my boy, time's up."

JACOPO PONTORMO, "ST JOHN THE EVANGELIST"

(CHURCH OF SANTA FELICITA,

BARBADORI-CAPPONI CHAPEL)

VASARI'S CORRIDOR

The custodian was waiting at the agreed location in front of a large door. A metallic jangling of keys, the dull click of a lock, a sinister creaking… and the door closed itself behind them.

"And where are we now?" Philip asked, hit by a wave of fresh air.

A long stairway stretched before them, its walls covered with paintings. The stairs ended at a long corridor—and that, too, was covered with pictures.

"In just a minute we'll be over the Ponte Vecchio. This is the corridor that Cosimo I had his trusted architect Giorgio Vasari build as a wedding gift for his son, Francesco. It was finished in just five months."

"Nice present."

"A genuine 'prince's passageway.' The corridor is a kilometre long, and allowed him to move quickly between the government seat at the Palazzo Vecchio and his home at Palazzo Pitti, without setting foot among the common folk. There was always the risk of being attacked."

"It crosses right over the Ponte Vecchio?"

"That's right: the corridor rests *on water and air*, as Vasari himself proudly described. It actually passes over the goldsmiths' shops, except for the last section, where the tower-house of the Mannelli family stands. The tower was built during the Middle Ages to protect the bridge. The corridor was supposed to cross through it, but— prince or no prince—the Mannelli wouldn't give their permission, and they had to make the corridor go around it."

"I think I remember seeing this corridor somewhere else… In some old movie, maybe."

"That's my boy! The movie you remember is *Paisà* by Roberto Rossellini. It tells six stories from the liberation of Italy during World War II. In one of the scenes, members of the resistance use the corridor to cross the river without being detected by the Germans."

JACOPO PONTORMO, "THE DEPOSITION"

"And what about the paintings?"

"Oh, they're actually very valuable stuff. We're on the section above the bridge where the collection of self-portraits is kept—and that's more than seven hundred paintings!"

"It's funny to see them all lined up like this: one is done head-on, another in the mirror, one in artsy clothing, another in evening wear… They're holding different things in their hands, too: flowers, a brush, a book, even a skull!"

"Look at the view from these little 'portholes:' streets, houses… You can even stick your nose into the church of Santa Felicita!"

"I can relate to Cosimo. You really do feel like a king here, up above the city, hidden from sight: you can keep your eye on everything."

"Now, get ready," Uncle Charlie called from the end of the corridor. "After the room of wonders, you're in for the garden of wonders: Boboli!"

BOBOLI GARDENS

"I promised you grottoes, and here's a spectacular one. What do you think?"

They were standing in front of Buontalenti's Grotto. Statues of sheep and shepherds peeped out here and there among the rocks, and exotic animals were frescoed on the walls. Copies of Michelangelo's *Prisoners* lay concealed under cascades of realistic stalactites. Sunbeams entered through an opening in the grotto's ceiling and reflected off a large glass basin full of water. The reflections danced off the stalactites creating bizarre, surreal light effects.

169 JACOPO PONTORMO, "THE ANGEL GABRIEL"

"It's an extraordinary spot. Buontalenti worked on it for ten years! The idea was to coax the grace of living creatures out of a coarse material—the stalactites. The sculpted figures are like a middle ground between stone and life."

"Cool. Looks like a set from a fantasy movie."

"And it wouldn't be complete without the water games that were so popular back then."

"Who's the fatso on the turtle over there?"

"That's the fountain of the *Bacchino*, or 'Little Bacchus,' and the chubby fellow is Morgante, a character Cosimo was very fond of."

"You were absolutely right about this place. It's fantastic."

"But you ain't seen nothing yet! Come on, you've won yourself a pit stop."

An steep boulevard led them up to a tall red pavilion crowned with a small dome.

"This is the Kaffeehaus, one of Grand Duke Peter Leopold's favourite places. He would sit here sipping his hot chocolate and enjoying the view. You know, just like that."

"I think I had about enough at Rivoire's. I'll take an orange soda."

They sat at one of the small tables lining the avenue. Uncle Charlie took advantage of the break to give his nephew an overview of the garden's history.

"Back when the Pitti family owned the place, there were only olive and fruit trees on this hill. Then Eleonora de Toledo, Cosimo's wife, bought the palace and moved the family here. Result: the entire hill behind the palace was transformed into a colossal stage for the pastimes and diversions of the royal court. It was the first time that anyone had planted such a large and diverse garden: there was the 'secret garden,' with medicinal and poisonous plants, hedge labyrinths…"

170

"FORT BELVEDERE & PITTI," ONE OF THE FAMOUS LUNETTES BY JUSTUS UTENS, A FLEMISH PAINTER (BORN IN BRUSSELS) WHO IN THE LATER 16TH CENTURY PORTRAYED FOURTEEN MEDICI VILLAS

(BUT PERHAPS YOU'VE BOUGHT THE POSTER SHOWING THE WHOLE LOT!)

BELVEDER CON PITTI

"Where maybe they'd get lost!"

"Sure, and on purpose, too. That way someone would have to come looking for them. Expert gardeners—not quite as skilled as Edward Scissorhands, but just about— pruned the hedges into the shapes of animals, heroes and fearful monsters. Water, with its pleasant and relaxing gurgle, ran though stone canals to finally spew out from fountains or from the mouths of large sculpted masks. Fountains sprayed drops to the sky with effects that you can well imagine—all the colours of the rainbow."

"Not bad."

"Now that we're rested up, let's continue our exploration."

Another uphill stretch led them to the statue of *Abundance*.

"We're now directly beneath the bastions of Fort Belvedere. The Medici had it built this high up for defence reasons. In case of popular revolt, all they'd have to do to get from Palazzo Pitti to the fortress was cross their garden: a matter of minutes."

"They must have had something on their conscience: they were always thinking about ways to escape."

"Not so much escaping as defending themselves. The cannons of the fort were always aimed in towards the city: that way, the Florentines would think twice before rising up against the Medici."

© GIAMBOLOGNA & PIETRO TACCA

"The power of persuasion!"

A short descent brought them to Neptune's *Vivaio* or 'Fish Reserve.' In the middle, a large statue of the sea god emerged from the water, trident in hand.

"Here they used to raise fish destined for the grand dukes' dinner table. That's how it got its name."

They continued downhill and reached the long, cypress-lined avenue known as the *Viottolone*.

"Either side of the boulevard," Uncle Charlie explained, "there's a number of narrow paths covered with closely meshed plant arbours, known as *cerchiate*.

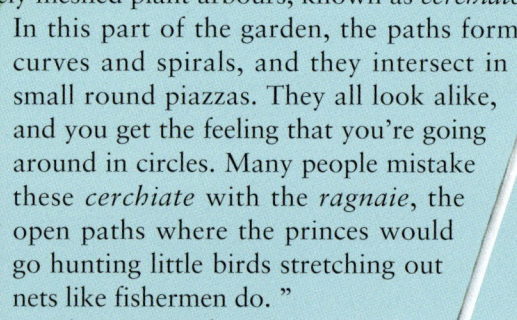

In this part of the garden, the paths form curves and spirals, and they intersect in small round piazzas. They all look alike, and you get the feeling that you're going around in circles. Many people mistake these *cerchiate* with the *ragnaie*, the open paths where the princes would go hunting little birds stretching out nets like fishermen do. "

"That's a nice fountain... And there's an island in the middle!"

"In fact, it's called the Isolotto, or 'Little Island.' The obligatory statue of Neptune is there in the middle. The four statues at his feet represent the great rivers known at the time: the Nile, Euphrates, Tiber and Ganges.

172

Then there's the island itself, lush with plant life. They choose the flower varieties carefully in such a way that there's always something in bloom."

At the end of another path lay the Amphitheatre.

"They used to hold plays here, and extravagant parties. And, of course, Buontalenti's fireworks were always in demand. On special occasions and whenever foreign royalty visited, they held parades with allegorical floats and military displays. And hold on to your hat: that's a real Egyptian obelisk! It comes from the temple of Amon in Luxor—an old buddy of mine… It dates back to 1500 years before Christ, give or take a year. The big stone basin, on the other hand, is Roman, and was taken from the Baths of Caracalla."

"We've come a long way," Philip commented, indicating the green dome of the Kaffeehaus, small in the distance.

AMMANNATI'S COURTYARD

"So, did you like Boboli?"

"I've seen better… Just kidding, it was great. And now?"

"One last push: I want to show you Palazzo Pitti's courtyard. We'll see the Palatine Gallery in the next couple of days when we have more time."

Philip and his uncle descended down a covered passageway and entered the palace courtyard.

"It was designed by Bartolomeo Ammannati. The princes used it for their parties and games."

"Not exactly workaholics, were they? It sounds like non-stop partying around here!"

"Picture this: one time they lined the courtyard with wooden beams waterproofed with pitch and filled it with water to wage a naval battle!"

"Like the Romans did at the Colosseum."

On the occasion of the wedding of Ferdinando de' Medici and Christine of Lorraine, in 1589, the courtyard of Palazzo Pitti was flooded with water for a 'naumachia,' or naval battle (below, in an engraving by Orazio Scarabelli, in the Uffizi). The idea was borrowed from the ancient Romans: the Colosseum was equipped with an hydraulic system specially designed for such battles—but the gladiators really killed each other!

"Exactly. And look: see the statue of Hercules at the end of the left-hand loggia? There's a bas-relief with the portrait of a donkey. They called her the *muletta*: she carried the stone and wooden beams they used to construct the courtyard, and worked so hard that she died as soon as it was finished."

"Poor thing… But still, I don't suppose many donkeys get a monument made after them."

"I wouldn't be so sure…" Uncle Charlie mused, smoothing his beard.

Palazzo Pitti's Façade

Philip hadn't realized how enormous the stone façade of the palace was until they were outside. The sloping square in front of the building seemed almost dwarfed by it.

"Now that I've seen its façade, I can understand why Tuscan rulers from the Medici on wanted to use this as their royal palace."

"The building didn't always look this way. It all started in the mid 1400s with a wealthy banker named Luca Pitti. He

174

was one of the first to have a palace built on this side of the Arno, and commissioned the design to the usual Brunelleschi. The architect died before it was finished though, and left the project in the hands of his favourite pupil, Luca Fancelli, who followed the maestro's original sketches. The façade is made up of enormous, roughly hewn blocks of stone, and is much more 'rustic' than others of the same period."

"Incredible. Seen up close, it looks like the wall of a quarry!"

"The building that Brunelleschi envisioned was only seven windows long—those ones in the middle. The façade, however, was, designed to be *expandable*."

"How do you mean?"

"The two vertical stripes on the façade alternate in a regular pattern. Looking from top to bottom: first you have window-window-little window, then window-window-*big* window. If the owner happened to feel like expanding the palace, all he'd have to do was add more strips on either side respecting the pattern: one strip of one type, one strip of the other."

"Such a grand façade must have been amazing publicity for Luca Pitti."

"And, like the good banker he was, Luca didn't like risks. That's why he had all the houses at the bottom of the square torn down… just in case people couldn't properly view his little gem!"

ARNO & OLTRARNO

THE ARNO RIVER

iulia was curled up in an easy chair, leafing through (surprise surprise) a fashion magazine. "Philip, you've been in Florence for days and we still haven't talked about the Arno and its bridges. Why don't we start the day with a little walk down the river banks?"

"Sounds good to me."

"Excellent," Uncle Charles agreed, stretched out on the bed with his laptop. "Just give me a minute to finish this game… Queen takes Bishop…"

THE ARNO RIVER

"We can follow the Lungarno della Zecca all the way up to Ponte Vecchio, and return along the other side."

"Right!" Charles crowed, disconnecting from the ICC (and visibly satisfied with the outcome of the game). "We'll take Philip to see the Specola. As for you, Giulia," he continued casting a disapproving glance at the fashion magazine, "why don't you put that *thing* down and tell Philip a little about Florence's relationship with the river?"

"We were waiting for you, if I'm not mistaken," Giulia retorted with a sour little smile. "And for your information—oh well, never mind. Anyway, Philip, Florentines nowadays have a fairly remote connection to the river, but it wasn't always that way. My grandfather used to swim in it. On Sundays in the summertime, he and his parents would picnic on the shore, and he'd play in the gravel just as you would at the beach."

"*And you in poems shall live forever, banks that the Arno greets in passing...*" Uncle Charlie intoned. "The Italian poet Ugo Foscolo, my dears: he dedicated this sonnet to a young and lovely Florentine girl he was in love with... And speaking of literature: the great Mark Twain wrote that in order to be able to call the Arno a real river, they'd have to pump some more water into it. Well, he should have been here on 4 November 1966," he added with a snort. "He would have sung a different tune!"

The Flood

"That's when the famous flood hit?"

"That's right," Giulia resumed, giving her friend a dirty look. "I was the one telling the story, wasn't I? The river flooded the entire historic centre, devastating libraries, museums, invaluable archives, churches, schools and shops. To say nothing of the houses: entire blocks underwater, families left homeless... some people even lost their lives."

"Were you in school at the time?"

"No, I was still too young. Anyway, it was a holiday, fortunately, and all the children were at home. People who were out of town when the flood hit had to wait for days before they were able to contact their loved ones. My aunt's boyfriend thought about going to find her in a rowboat! Fortunately, they were able stop him. Just imagine: in some neighbourhoods, the floodwater was more than five metres deep!"

"It happened all at once, just like that?"

"Actually, it had been raining for several days beforehand. The Arno was swollen with run-off from its tributaries, which were full to capacity. But that had happened before, and no one was expecting catastrophe to strike. That fateful night, the river was hit with run-off from the Valdarno levees: they were near the bursting point, and technicians were forced to open the bulkheads. It was the proverbial last straw: in the first light of dawn, the water released from the levees hit the city. The Arno overflowed its banks and invaded the streets."

"A river of mud!"

"Worse. As water flooded the city's basements, it ripped out heating systems and oil tanks. A slimy, foul-smelling torrent mixed in with the mud. For many years afterwards, a black line of oil remained on the façades of houses and monuments where the water level had reached its highest—a

sobering reminder of that terrible night."

"What did people do?"

"Electricity, water, telephones… nothing was working. Lots of people were trapped in their houses and the city was isolated from the rest of the world. Once they were safe from the furious torrent, there was nothing anybody could do but gather around their windows and watch: cars that had been parked

outside were dragged away by the current, crashing against one side of the street and then the other…"

"There were also acts of heroism," Charles interrupted. "The inmates of the old Murate Prison behind Santa Croce helped bring the guards' families to safety. Some apparently even managed to escape by swimming across the flooded river!"

"Judging by your description, it's a miracle that more masterpieces weren't destroyed like Cimabue's was," Philip murmured, wide-eyed.

"The worst was averted by the quick thinking of various museum employees. They carried the most important pieces to the upper floors. That's how Filippo Lippi's *Coronation* was saved, for example—it was being restored in the Uffizi at the time. They rescued Galileo's telescopes too—the ones you saw at the Museum of the History of Science. The tiles on the doors of the baptistery, on the other hand, were saved by the bars on the gates that had been put up to protect them. The violent force of the water dislodged them, but wasn't able to wash them away. People came in from all over the world to help save the treasures of the National Central Library, which is located on the banks of the Arno, and partially underneath it. Richard Burton was among them: remember, Charles?"

WEIRS & MILLS

"Now and then, however, the Arno plays some nice surprises. I remember a particularly cold winter: we woke up one day and found the river completely frozen over—there were people ice-skating on it! You see that sort of wall that comes up to water level, crossing from one bank to the other? That's one of two weirs in Florence marking the extremes of the medieval

city. They're built in such a way as to create small, artificial lakes, so that during summer drought periods, people could still fish and have enough water for their daily needs. There's a street called Via dei Renai, or 'Sandbank Street' on the other shore, where they used to collect river sand to make mortar. There used to be several mills located at this point, their blades powered by the current."

"What did they need mills for?"

"Their wheels powered the *gualchiere*, machines that helped waterproof the fabrics by beating them vigorously in tubs full of water and… pee. That was one of the best-kept secrets of the Florentine wool industry, which was famous throughout the world."

When they reached the Ponte Vecchio, Philip noticed something strange. "Giulia, why are most of the houses on either side of the bridge so modern-looking?"

THE BRIDGES OF FLORENCE

"Towards the end of World War II, Florence, like many other Italian cities, was occupied by German troops. They were retreating to the North, pressured by the advancing Allied forces. As they were pulling out of Florence, the Germans decided to blow up the city's bridges in order to slow their enemies' progress."

"The Allies were coming in from that direction," Charles explained, pointing south towards the Oltrarno (which, by the way, means 'beyond the Arno').

"And they blew up all the bridges?!"

"All but one. All Florentine bridges are modern except for the Ponte Vecchio and the Santa Trinita bridge. The Germans were kind enough to leave the Ponte Vecchio intact, but in compensation they blew up the streets approaching it on

either side. My mother still remembers it: Via Por Santa Maria and Via Guicci-ardini were reduced to a mountain of rubble."

"But if Ponte Vecchio was the only bridge the Germans spared, why is the Santa Trinita bridge still standing?"

"The stones were fished out of the river one by one, and the entire bridge rebuilt. The statues of the Seasons that are on each corner of the bridge were re-covered and restored. The only piece that wasn't found right away was Spring's head: it showed up several years later. Anyway, the bridges of Florence were destroyed and rebuilt on more than one occasion. The Ponte Vecchio was period-ically washed away by floods until they figured out a way to make it more resist-ant. The bridge used to be the site of tanning shops, butchers, blacksmiths… All very picturesque: too bad they used the river as a dump! At the end of the 1500s, Grand Duke Ferdinando decided to reserve the bridge for goldsmiths' shops, who would presumably pollute the river less. They're still there."

"What's the bridge after Santa Trinita called?"

"The Carraia Bridge. It was named for the carts that were used to carry the wool that was dyed in San Fredi-ano over to the city centre, on the other side of the river. It was originally built out of wood with stone pylons. The friars of the nearby convent of Ognissanti were responsible for its maintenance, and were supposed to defend it in case of enemy attack. One time during the Middle Ages, they organized a big event there. The theme was Hell, and they launched a raft with actors dressed as devils. There were fireworks, trumpets, drums… you can imagine the scene. Anyway, the event attracted so many spectators that the bridge collapsed and a lot of people drowned. As a consequence, the citizens decided they would never build anoth-er wooden bridge."

THE OLTRARNO

"Pardon me for interrupting my lecture," Giulia said, "but we have already crossed the Ponte Vecchio, and if we keep on going we'll wind up back at Palazzo Pitti. But I have to deliver this package at all costs."

"What package?" Charles and Philip asked in unison.

"The ceramic vase I've got in my backpack. My cat knocked it over and it shattered: Mario's the only one who can save it!"

"In the Oltrarno," Uncle Charlie explained, "there are artisans who work downright miracles with a whole variety of materials: leather, silver, bronze, marble, semi-precious stone, wood, paper… and ceramic, of course. There are fewer pizza parlours and ice-cream shops than there are in the centre, but you can visit workshops where colourful characters live and work: woodcarvers, cabinet-makers, goldsmiths, restorers…"

"And here's one of them," announced Giulia, pointing at a Mario's workshop.

'Signor Mario' was a renowned marble and ceramics restorer. He proved to be a very kind and patient fellow, and showed Philip some interesting tricks of the trade: the paste he used for gluing the pieces together, those used to patch the missing sections, paintbrushes and colours, the kiln and even a sampling of wax models used to recreate the hands, feet and legs of broken ancient statues. Busts, scalpels and chunks of marble of every size littered the workshop. It was, to put it mildly, a real mess.

"What a great place," Philip admired. "Reminds me of my bedroom."

Giulia left her vase in Mario's capable hands, and the three proceeded without further ado to the Specola Museum.

YOUNG PETER LEOPOLD OF HABSBURG-LORRAINE IN A PORTRAIT BY BACCIARELLI...

THE SPECOLA MUSEUM

"What does *specola* mean?" Philip asked.

"It comes from a Latin word meaning observatory, and in fact it refers to a building from which they study the stars."

"You told me it was a museum of natural history…"

"It is. In 1775, Grand Duke Peter Leopold founded the Museum of Natural History. Then, at the end of the century, they added the astronomical observatory."

"It's pretty old museum."

"That's part of its charm."

"The zoological section of the Specola," Giulia said, "hosts a vast assortment of stuffed animals, specimens of an incredibly wide array of creatures. The other section is dedicated to a formidable collection of anatomical models in wax. It's one of the most important in the world in terms of quantity and quality."

Philip inspected creatures of every shape and size: tropical butterflies with enormous multicoloured wings, gigantic beetles, minuscule hummingbirds and sinister sharks.

"Look here, Giulia!" Philip blurted. "These giant sea turtles are like the ones Darwin studied for his theory of evolution! I read about them in school last year. They lived on those islands in the Pacific Ocean: the Gu… Go…"

"Galapagos."

"And what did I say?"

"Come check this out: there's something in here I think you'll find interesting."

"A computer!"

"Push the button that corresponds to a certain animal, and the software will give you

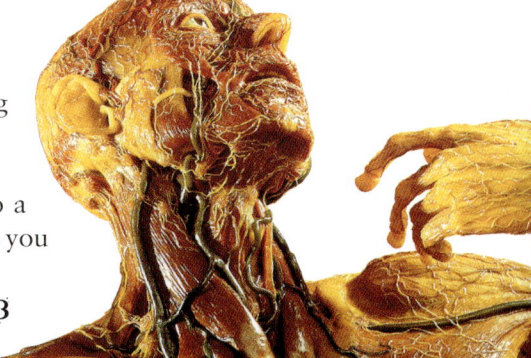

information about its habits and habitat—if it still exists. And listen: it even plays the animal's call!"

"And here's the wax section, straight out of a vintage horror movie. These reproductions are exceptionally realistic, and the Florentines have always been rightfully proud of them. Many have tried to copy them, but nobody has come anywhere close to this kind of result. An enormous amount of work went into each model: outstanding artists drew the designs from real, dissected corpses, and equally skilled sculptors then modelled them in wax. In order to make the small blood vessels, or capillaries… How many capillaries are there, Philip?"

"Capillaries? The exact number? I would say… a whole bunch."

"Give or take a couple… To reproduce them accurately, they used silk or metal thread, coated in wax and applied one by one with tweezers."

"Don't flatter yourself. I know perfectly well why you're telling me all these gory details."

"What do you mean?"

"You're hoping I'll lose my appetite!"

"I've always been a sucker for lost causes."

THE CHURCH OF SANTO SPIRITO

Once they had finished at the mandatory *trattoria*, Giulia chose their next stop. "Let's go visit Santo Spirito. It's one of my favourite churches."

ADRIANA SILVESTRI, 1999

"This is yet another one of Brunelleschi's works," Uncle Charlie began when they were outside the church, "but unlike San Lorenzo, it wasn't built the way he had hoped. He wanted the façade facing the Arno, looking out over a square bordering the river. In those days, it was still possible to navigate the Arno—the effect would have been spectacular!"

"So why didn't they do it that way in the end?"

"Because this plan conflicted with the interests of various families that owned houses and shops in the area. There were other differences as well: the exterior walls of the church were supposed to ripple, following on the outside the line of the semicircular chapels that are inside, in the side aisles. This line of chapels was to continue along the interior façade, as well as in the transept and choir. The idea was to have an uninterrupted portico around a central, luminous nave. Unfortunately, there weren't any architects who had the courage to follow Brunelleschi's instructions: the exterior walls, which were supposed to be curved, were left straight, and the two naves were never brought together."

"This church doesn't have a façade either."

"That's true up to a certain point. There was one night when it had at least a hundred of them, one right after the next," Giulia chimed in. "A few years ago, a Florentine artist organized a singular kind of competition. Each participant proposed a decorated façade for the church. Artists from all over the world participated, and their designs were projected onto the existing façade. The effect was amazing: the projects ranged from serious to funny, mysterious, provocative… In one of the bars around the piazza there's a whole room devoted to that night—its walls are covered with pics of the most promising designs."

"By the way," Uncle Charlie noted as they were leaving the piazza, "did you know that—along with the various churches and buildings he designed—Brunelleschi also built fortifications throughout Tuscany? He did some in Rimini and Pesaro, too. At a certain point, it seems that they even pulled him into a scheme to turn the city of Lucca into an island. He was supposed to built a dyke and deviate the course of the Arno…"

© MASOLINO DA PANICALE

THE BRANCACCI CHAPEL

"And now," Charles continued, "I suggest we pay a call to our friend Masaccio."

'Masaccio…' Philip pondered as they entered the church of the Carmine. 'Let's see what he came up with this time.'

"He really outdid himself here," Uncle Charlie promised. "He and Masolino frescoed an entire chapel."

"Back with Masolino again!"

"Actually, we don't know if Masaccio was called in by Felice Brancacci to finish Masolino's work," Giulia clarified, "or if they worked side by side. The usual debate over who painted what resulted in sleepless nights for generations of scholars. But really, it's not so hard to distinguish them. Masolino paints graceful and dreamy characters, while Masaccio is more realistic, more careful with the anatomy, volume and expression of his characters. To see the difference in style, all you have to do is look at their ren-ditions of Adam and Eve. Masolino did the *Temptation* and Masaccio, the *Expulsion from Paradise*. Look here: Masolino's couple is delicate and elegant, almost angelic. Masaccio, on the other hand, represents them after the fall, and he goes in for the drama: bodies bent under the weight of their shame, faces like masks of pain… He's able to convey their an-

guish through movements and gestures: a truly remarkable realism."

"Masaccio didn't draw his figures with simple lines," Uncle Charlie interrupted, wanting to put his two-cents in. "He constructed them with contrasts of light and shadow. And the brushstrokes of colour aren't all nice and tidy, but sure, broad and easy—used sparingly, but to wonderful effect. This way, the fresco looks almost three-dimensional."

"Like in Ghirlandaio's frescoes," Giulia continued, "the sacred stories unfold not in some imaginary setting of the past, but rather in the Tuscan countryside or in the streets of Florence. They're skilfully reproduced with the help of perspective, and an eye to detail: the narrow streets, the houses with their projections, elegant

© MASACCIO

palaces and the wash hanging out to dry… Look at the crowd witnessing the miracles: the merchants, the needy and ill waiting to be cured by St Peter—he's the protagonist of these stories. In short, your attention is drawn not to the incredible and miraculous, but rather to the gestures and expressions of the individual characters. Take, for example, the scene of the *Tribute Money*…"

"Hold it right there," Philip barked. "I don't know what you're talking about."

"The story's right out of the Gospel. Jesus is about to enter a city when he's stopped by a tax collector who demands tribute money. Bowing to mortal law, Je-

© FILIPPINO LIPPI

sus sends Peter to the lake: there he finds a fish with the silver coin they needed in its mouth. Now, you'd think that the scene would revolve around this extraordinary fish: instead, Masaccio puts the emphasis on the people. These are authentic portraits, that bring to mind Donatello's sculpture or ancient Roman reliefs: figures so solemn and majestic, the likes of them had never been seen before."

"You remember Gentile da Fabriano?" Charles asked. "Forget all about him. Here the body is no

longer a surface but a solid entity, so realistic that it casts a shadow on the ground. And speaking of shadow: in the fresco, the light source that illuminates the scene is located to the upper right, which is exactly where real light enters through the window in the chapel. What's more, Masaccio painted the mountains in the background using aerial perspective—he lightened their shade little by little, thus simulating the effect of the atmosphere on distant objects. We saw that technique used by Leonardo."

"Slow down. You're losing me."

"In the meantime, why don't you give us a little recap of everything we've said so far," Uncle Charlie teased.

"Solid, anatomically convincing figures arranged in a clear, controlled space, illuminated by a coherent light source."

Giulia and Charles gawked at him with their mouths hanging open.

"Had you there for a minute. I just read that in the guide. Go ahead."

"It's the same issue we were talking about with the *Trinity*," Giulia explained. "The figures of Masolino are creations of fantasy, removed from the real world. With Masaccio, on the other hand, the painting becomes a window beyond which the real world continues—same space, same light, same perspective. Western art would follow in his footsteps for four hundred years."

"Masaccio pursued the path of realism that Giotto had embarked upon. His work influenced at least two generations of artists. The most important painters of the mid 1400s—Filippo Lippi, Fra Angelico, Andrea del Castagno and Piero della Francesca—all looked to him for inspiration. But his influence really blossomed with the generation that followed: Leonardo, Michelangelo, Raphael… It's no coincidence that Michelangelo's first drawings were sketches of the characters in the *Tribute* scene…"

FRESCO

MURAL PAINTINGS ARE ONLY CALLED 'FRES-
COES' IF THE PAINT HAS BEEN APPLIED DIRECT-
LY ONTO FRESH PLASTER. THEY ARE DIFFICULT
TO RECOGNISE WITH THE NAKED EYE, BUT IN
GENERAL FRESCOES ARE BRIGHTER AND BETTER
PRESERVED THAN MURALS PAINTED 'A SECCO.'

THE PROCEDURE IS RATHER LENGTHY. FIRST
OF ALL, THE ARTIST CHOOSES THE WALL AND
SPREADS ONTO IT THE FIRST LAYER OF PLAS-
TER, CONSISTING OF LIME AND SAND MIXED
WITH WATER. THEN HE HAS TO WAIT FOR THE
PLASTER TO BE COMPLETELY DRY, WHICH TAKES
SEVERAL MONTHS. MEANWHILE, WITH A RED
PASTEL CALLED 'SINOPIA' THE PAINTER MAKES
A DRAWING WHICH HELPS HIM TO DISTRIBUTE

© MASACCIO

© MASOLINO DA PANICALE

HIS DESIGN OVER THE SPACE AVAILABLE, AND
TO WORK OUT HOW MUCH CAN BE PAINTED IN
A SINGLE DAY. THIS LATTER INFORMATION
IS PARTICULARLY IMPORTANT, BECAUSE THE
FRESCO MUST BE PAINTED ON PLASTER THAT IS
STILL FRESH, I.E. DAMP, AND SO THE PAINTER
WILL SPREAD THE SECOND, THINNER LAYER OF
PLASTER—THE LAYER HE IS GOING TO PAINT
ON—ONLY ON THE AREA HE EXPECTS TO FINISH
BY THE EVENING. SINCE THE PLASTER APPLIED
ON A GIVEN DAY OVERLAPS A LITTLE BIT WITH
THE PREVIOUS DAY'S PLASTER, IT IS POSSIBLE
TO DETERMINE THE NUMBER OF 'PATCHES' AND
THUS THE NUMBER OF WORKING DAYS SPENT
ON THE FRESCO. FROM THE LATE 15TH CENTURY
PAINTERS PREFERRED TO APPLY THE DRAWING
DIRECTLY TO THE SECOND LAYER OF PLAS-
TER BY MEANS OF THE 'PERFORATED PATTERN'
TECHNIQUE.

THIS IS HOW IT IS DONE:

(a) TAKE A SHEET OF PAPER THE SAME SIZE AS THE FRESCO YOU WANT TO PAINT, AND DRAW THE DESIGN ON IT;

(b) USING A LARGE NEEDLE PRICK HUNDREDS OF HOLES ALONG THE LINES IN THE DRAWING;

(c) FIX THE PAPER ONTO THE FRESH PLASTER, AND BEAT IT WITH A CANVAS CUSHION FILLED WITH POWDERED CHARCOAL: THE POWDER PASSES THROUGH THE NEEDLE-HOLES AND TRACES THE OUTLINE OF THE DRAWING ONTO THE WALL.

THE NEXT STEP IS TO PAINT ON THE COLOURS, WHICH IN THOSE DAYS WERE OBTAINED FROM EARTHS, PLANTS OR STONES, WHICH HAD TO BE GROUND UP AND MIXED WITH WATER.

MAKE SURE YOU DON'T HAVE ANY SECOND THOUGHTS—OTHERWISE, YOU'LL HAVE TO SCRAPE OFF THE PLASTER AND START ALL OVER AGAIN!

© MASACCIO

© MASACCIO & FILIPPINO LIPPI

AT PALAZZO PITTI

THE PALATINE GALLERY

he next morning at ten o'clock, Philip, Giulia and Charles climbed the monumental staircase of Palazzo Pitti, headed for the Palatine Gallery.

"Its real name," Uncle Charlie explained, "was *quadreria*. That's because between the 17th and the 18th century the rooms that had once served as reception halls gradually filled up with the grand-ducal collection of *quadri*, or paintings. They weren't displayed in chronological order, though, the way they are at the Uffizi. They were arranged according to purely scenographic criteria."

"What do you mean?"

"The walls are tapestried in red silk and lined up to the ceiling with paintings in precious, gilded frames. The shapes, sizes, and even subjects of the paintings correspond perfectly to those on the opposite wall, symmetrical as the wings of a butterfly. The ceiling is decorated with frescoes and white or gilded stuccoes. The museum remains precisely as it was arranged back then. Some of the paintings were even 'hinged' to the walls, like cabinet doors, so that people could tilt them as they wished and view them in the best available light!"

"It's a little like the Stibbert Museum," Philip observed. "Looking at the works of art, you understand a lot about the tastes of their owners."

They entered a large, luminous hall. The Boboli Gardens could be seen out of the windows, and in the middle of the room stood an enormous round table.

"The whole thing is pieced together in semi-precious stones, on a blue background of lapis lazuli," Giulia noted. "It shows Apollo surrounded by the symbols of the Muses."

"I know who that is," Philip exclaimed. "Apollo was the Greek god of the sun."

"He was also crazy about music. The Muses were the goddesses of Olympus

'responsible' for the arts and sciences. Not coincidentally, the word 'museum' derives from Greek and means 'shrine dedicated to the Muses'."

"This table," the archaeologist declared, "is the point of departure for an artistic journey. It invites us to follow the road indicated by Apollo."

"And we shall boldly follow it."

"After you: first door on the left."

THE ROOMS OF THE PLANETS

The next room they entered was magnificently decorated with frescoes and stuccoes.

"This is the Room of Venus. Grand Duke Ferdinando II hired Pietro da Cortona to fresco the ceilings of five whole rooms illustrating the various phases of the education of a prince. In the oval portraits over there, you see Ferdinando and the future Cosimo III. But let's take things in order and start with the frescoes. In the middle of the ceiling there's Minerva, the one with the helmet. Minerva was the Latin name for Athena, the goddess of wisdom. She's grabbing a blond young man dressed in orange from the arms of Venus, the goddess of love. Ignoring the protests of Cupid (another god of love), Minerva pushes the boy towards Hercules—the brawny hero with the club and lion's skin. What could it all mean?"

"It means that the prince is getting a little too old to be lounging about all the time, and that it's time he started working out."

"Bodybuilding aside… the future grand duke had to apply himself to his studies so that one day he'd be able to enter public life and become a real man, like Hercules."

"I figured as much. But wait a minute. Why is Cupid always shown as a little boy?"

"He's a Peter Pan sort of figure. His mother Venus lets him play all the time and he never grows up. Speaking of Venus, there's a statue of her in the middle of the room—half-naked as usual, just getting out of the bathtub…"

"Is it an ancient sculpture?"

"No, but the fellow who sculpted it was very nostalgic for antiquity. It's the famous *Venus Italica* by Antonio Canova. He

RIGHT, A FAMOUS PORTRAIT BY TITIAN, THE GREAT PAINTER OF THE VENETIAN SCHOOL. THE MODEL OF THE PAINTING IS KNOWN UNDER VARIOUS NAMES: "THE MAN WITH GREY EYES", "THE ENGLISHMAN", "THE DUKE OF NORFOLK"—MEANING SIMPLY THAT WE DON'T HAVE A CLUE AS TO WHO THE GUY REALLY WAS. IF YOU LIKE TITIAN, THIS IS THE RIGHT PLACE TO BE: IN THE GALLERY YOU WILL FIND "THE CONCERTO", "MARY MAGDALEN", "LA BELLA" AND THE PORTRAITS OF TOMMASO MOSTI (A FELLOW SLIGHTLY RESEMBLING KEANU REEVES), PIETRO ARETINO AND IPPOLITO DE' MEDICI. NOT TO MENTION THE PAINTINGS HOUSED AT THE UFFIZI: "THE SICK MAN", "FLORA", THE PORTRAITS OF FRANCESCO DELLA ROVERE AND ELEONORA GONZAGA AND THE WORLD-FAMOUS "VENUS OF URBINO." MANY OF THESE MASTERPIECES WERE THE PRIVATE POSSESSION OF THE DUKES OF URBINO, THE DELLA ROVERE FAMILY. THE LAST DESCENDANT OF THEIR LINE, VITTORIA, DAUGHTER OF FEDERICO DELLA ROVERE AND CLAUDIA DE' MEDICI, MARRIED FERDINANDO II OF TUSCANY: THUS THE MEDICI ACQUIRED NOT ONLY THE DUCHY OF URBINO, BUT A FAIR AMOUNT OF PAINTINGS AND OTHER, LET'S SAY, 'VALUABLE' ARTEFACTS.

was a great Neoclassical sculptor from the 1800s. The next room is dedicated to Apollo: the god is seated in the clouds and shows our boy a globe with the signs of the Zodiac. He's careful to point out Capricorn, whose influence Cosimo (the first grand duke) was born under. See, in the meantime the boy has grown up, and his hair has turned from blond to brown. Your turn!"

"What if he had red hair like me?"

"Philip…"

"All right, all right! I see it like this: it's a reminder that the prince is supposed to act like Cosimo."

"That's right. The prince must learn to manage his power and conquer Fame (the woman next to him with the trumpet). He's also supposed to promote the various arts. The upbringing of a prince was very important: he had to be a decent dancer, appreciate poetry and theatre, know enough about history to get by, and maybe even play a musical instrument. That's why the Muses are shown below. The third room is dedicated to Mars, and it's the most complicated. Mars, the god of war, is dressed like an ancient Roman, and offers his star at our little prince. He, in the meantime, has become a strapping, curly-headed youth, and he's busy hacking away at an enemy. The weapons of his fallen foes are gathered up by Hercules. On the other side, you see Victory crowned with laurel, separating the victors from the defeated, who are reduced to slavery. The winners are rewarded with coins and ears of wheat, the symbols of prosperity."

"Oh, happy day! The future grand duke's military service?"

"Let's just call it his training in warfare. Once sovereign, the young man would have to lead his people in battle."

"These people were such warmongers! Couldn't they just give peace a chance?"

"Apparently someone would have agreed with you," Giulia smiled. "You see that enormous painting occupying almost the entire wall in front of the window? It didn't wind up in this room by chance. The painting illustrates the *Consequences of War*, and was done by a Flemish painter named Rubens. He knew what he was talking about, too, as the Thirty Years' War was raging at the time—a terrible conflict that bloodied Europe from 1618 to 1648. The painting is read from left to right, and is so complex that when Rubens sent it to Tuscany, he felt obliged to include a letter of explanation. Let's see here. A woman exits the temple of Janus: she's dressed in mourning, dishevelled and in tears, howling her desperation. She represents Europe—you see the crown of towers on her head?—and her children are fighting among themselves. In the centre there's an incredible entanglement. Venus is trying in vain to keep Mars from fighting—Strife is stronger and drags him away. Mars' sword is covered in blood, and his foot is trampling a book."

"Because war kills culture."

"Precisely. The rampant violence also overwhelms three figures representing different aspects of devastation: the woman with the broken lute symbolizes shattered harmony; the mother and child represent the loss of innocent lives; the

THE ROOMS OF THE PLANETS

Raphael, "Madonna & Child with Young St John the Baptist" or "Madonna of the Chair" (c. 1516)

fallen man with compasses in his hand represents the utter destruction of the cities. Smoke rises from the battlefield—under Mars' sword you can make out knights in the distance—and two terrible monsters materialize in the top right-hand corner: Plague and Famine."

"No two ways about it: this Rubens character had some strong ideas."

"And now the last two episodes in the life of the future grand duke: the Rooms of Jupiter and Saturn. The Room of Jupiter used to be the throne room. In it, our prince is finally seen as a grown man—Hercules even hands over his club!—and he's being crowned by the king of the gods. And now, a dramatic turn of events: at this point in the story, Pietro da Cortona unexpectedly kicks the bucket."

"Right at the good part!"

"In the last room, the cycle was supposed to end with the death of the grand duke. This was a very dicey issue. To portray him as young and handsome was practically to wish him a premature death, while showing him as an old man you risked making him look worn-out and obsolete. Ciro Ferri was called in by the Medici to pick up where Pietro had left off, and he came up with an ingenious and diplomatic solution. The prince is led to Saturn, the one with the scythe in his hand, and acclaimed by Glory and Eternity. Hercules, the incarnation of the prince, climbs up on the grate—just like he does in the myth—and wins immortality. As you can see, Ciro's grand duke is ageless, so to speak: he's got white hair, but an athletic physique. Either he's young, in which case the white hair symbolizes wisdom; or else he's elderly, but still in great shape."

"Interesting…"

"That's all for today. What do you say we go catch a few rays in the Boboli? We can leave the 'Museo degli Argenti,' the Silver Museum, for tomorrow."

"Yes, sir!" Giulia and Philip barked in unison. Followed by "Just in time for a snack…" added by you-know-who.

AT PALAZZO PITTI (TAKE TWO)

THE SILVER MUSEUM

iulia had a conference to attend, so Philip and Charles returned to Palazzo Pitti on their own. "The Silver Museum—in Italian *Museo degli Argenti*," Uncle Charlie explained as they waited in line, "is called that because a section of the place was once used as a storeroom for objects that were crafted out of precious metals, but had subsequently gone out of style. They were stored here waiting to be either melted down or reused."

The line wasn't long, and after a few minutes the two entered the first room.

"I don't see much precious metal in here."

"Take a look at the walls."

The walls were covered in frescoes. The artist, Giovanni da San Giovanni, had transformed a room with vaulted ceiling into a sort of make-believe loggia. The columns were painted, as were the dusted stuccoes, and a procession wound its way through the architectural elements.

"This was the waiting room—the antechamber where people once waited to be received by the grand duke. Visitors would 'read' the walls to help pass the time, as comic books and magazines still hadn't been invented."

"Let me guess: the frescoes talk about the glory of the Medici family."

"Amazing—what gave it away? Yes, the frescoes celebrate the family, and in particular, of course, its most illustrious ancestor, Lorenzo the Magnificent. All the allegorical stuff is very complicated: Lorenzo

CATERINA DE' MEDICI IN A CAMEO OF ONYX, GOLD & RUBY

198

THE SILVER MUSEUM

is seen as the ideal politician, cunning but virtuous, and at the same time as the enlightened protector of philosophy and the arts, which had blossomed to an almost unprecedented extent during the Renaissance. There, look, that's him on the wall facing the entrance: he's the fellow with the slightly crooked nose, surrounded by various artists of his day. And—surprise surprise—the one showing him the freshly sculpted head of a faun is young Michelangelo."

THE DAUGHTER OF LORENZO DUKE OF URBINO, CATERINA DE' MEDICI PASSED HER CHILDHOOD IN A CONVENT. WHEN SHE WAS ONLY FOURTEEN, HER UNCLE, POPE CLEMENT VII, ARRANGED HER MARRIAGE WITH HENRY OF ORLÉANS, SON OF THE KING OF FRANCE FRANCIS I. THE LID OF THE CRYSTAL VASE ON THE RIGHT, THE WORK OF GASPARO MISERONI, BEARS THE INTERLOCKING INITIALS OF BRIDE AND GROOM (HC: HENRI & CATERINA). THE FORM OF THE HANDLE, HOWEVER, QUITE OPENLY ALLUDES TO HENRY'S 'OFFICIAL' LOVER, THE LOVELY DIANE OF POITIERS: THE CRESCENT MOON SCYTHE IS THE SYMBOL OF THE HUNTING GODDESS DIANA. IN FRANCE CATERINA WAS NOT EXACTLY WELCOME: THE ARISTOCRACY DESPISED HER (A BOURGEOIS!) AND FEARED HER CONNECTION WITH THE POPE. WHEN HENRY BECAME KING, CATERINA WAS SEQUESTERED IN THE CASTLE OF CHAUMONT, WHERE SHE SPENT THE FOLLOWING TWELVE YEARS. YET CHILDREN ARE BEING BORN—TEN OF THEM, AMONG WHICH THREE KINGS OF FRANCE (FRANCIS II, CHARLES IX & HENRY III), AS WELL AS THE FAMOUS REINE MARGOT, WHO WILL MARRY HENRY OF NAVARRE. THEN HENRY IS MORTALLY WOUNDED DURING A JOUST, AND CATERINA RISES TO POWER: THIRTY YEARS OF INTRIGUE AND CIVIL STRIFE AWAIT HER—THE DARK YEARS OF THE WARS OF RELIGION BETWEEN CATHOLICS AND HUGUENOTS.

"LORENZO SURROUNDED BY ARTISTS" BY OTTAVIO VANNINI

(ROOM IV, THE AUDIENCE ROOM)

A VIEW OF THE GRAND-DUCAL SQUARE
(I.E. PIAZZA DELLA SIGNORIA)

In the rooms that followed, Philip was delighted by the images on the walls: fantastic architecture populated with servants in full livery, children playing with little monkeys and parrots, young princes that inspected the visitor through their spyglasses…

"Starting with Cosimo the Elder, the Medici had always been great collectors. Every member of the family took it upon himself to add onto the collections he had inherited. These antique vases in semi-precious stone once belonged to Roman emperors. They were collected by Lorenzo, a fanatic of Ancient Rome, and they formed the original nucleus of Grand Duke Cosimo I's collection. Then came his son Francesco, who was obsessed with alchemy and hoped to find a way to transform lead into gold. He personally commissioned several other vases that were then added to the collection. There are vases in lapis lazuli and others in rock crystal. They look like blown glass, but instead were made from a single block of transparent quartz that skilled craftsmen were able to carve down to an incredible thinness.

BUONTALENTI

This lapis lazuli vase belonged to Francesco, and was designed for him by Bernardo Buontalenti, his inseparable partner in experiments. It's in the shape of a flask and the handles are two fantasy creatures, the harpies. The bird's body is made of stone, while the long snake's throat and fascinating woman's face are made in gold. And now look at that strange creature, half-woman half-fish, emerging from the vase: an endless golden neck extends from its curved bust; her head, too, is made of gold and glaze. If you look at her from above, you see a monstrous face with puffy cheeks and curved eyebrows; but if you look at her from below, you see the beautiful face of a siren—actually, the monster is the girl's hat! You know, monsters were very fashionable in Francesco's court, and Bernardo never missed an opportunity to depict them all over vases, armour, palaces, grottoes, and even under the windows of Florence. He loved blending reality with fantasy, the natural with the artificial…"

GALLERY OF MODERN ART & COSTUME GALLERY

"I see you still have a little spunk left in you," Uncle Charlie observed. "What do you say we hop up to the Gallery of Modern Art on the top floor of the palace? We'll get to see some Macchiaioli."

"And who would those be?"

"Follow me and you'll see for yourself."

THE "ROTONDA DI PALMIERI" BY GIOVANNI FATTORI (1866)

AT PALAZZO PITTI (TAKE TWO)

Uncle and nephew entered the gallery. They had just been through halls full of enormous paintings where miscellaneous heroes fought in every conceivable way, and were celebrated accordingly. All of a sudden, they found themselves in front of relatively small canvases depicting children, peasants, ploughs abandoned in the middle of fields and deserted beaches beaten by the wind.

"Weird," Philip commented. "After all those glorious scenes in costume, these little paintings seem so... out of place."

"These are the Macchiaioli I was telling you about—the name comes from the Italian *macchia*, or patch. People called them that out of disrespect—something like paint-blotchers. Instead, they were great innovators for their technique as well as their choice of subjects. They represented reality at its humblest, and preferred to paint out in the open rather than in an art studio, just as the French Impressionists did. Their painting also had a social side—look at their subjects: peasants, nannies, inmates, hospices..."

At the exit of the Palazzo, Philip noticed a sign pointing to the Costume Gallery. "What's this?"

"A nice little museum. Some of the exhibits change every two years: today, for example, you might find the costumes for an old-fashioned movie. Then there's the permanent exhibit with period clothing that goes from the beginning of the 1700s to the early 1900s. When you see those outfits full of lace, rigid supports, bows and counter-bows... I guarantee, you'll appreciate the comfort of today's clothing more than ever. Sure, the grand duke's wardrobe was more elegant than your Simpson's T-shirt... But I'd like to see him wearing it in this heat!"

Departure

At the Airport

iulia was driving her friends to the airport. An awkward silence hung in the car.

"There now," Uncle Charlie said with a certain embarrassment when the time had come to part ways. "It's not like we'll never see each other again. As a matter of fact, I was thinking of coming back in a couple of weeks. I still haven't heard anything from Egypt, and anyway it's always better to dig during the winter. How does that sound?"

"Terrific! I don't have any plans," Giulia replied, visibly excited.

Philip was reminded of the old adage that three's a crowd, and didn't quite know where to look.

"Here, this is for you." Giulia pulled a large package out of her backpack, and planted a smacking kiss on his cheek. "I hope you had a good time, and that we'll see each other again real soon…"

'What did she mean by that?' Philip thought to himself. 'Fifteen days isn't such a long time…'

Once they were airborne, Uncle Charlie gazed out the window with a thoughtful expression. Fluffy white clouds lazily were sliding by below them.

Florence (As It Was)

Philip, in the meantime, had opened his gift—a large book entitled *Florence. The Vanished City*. The book documented the massive demolition that took place during the late 1800s and transformed the medieval and Renaissance city into a modern and functional downtown. Philip leafed through the old photos with curiosity, trying to locate the places he had seen. It wasn't easy. The alleyways and

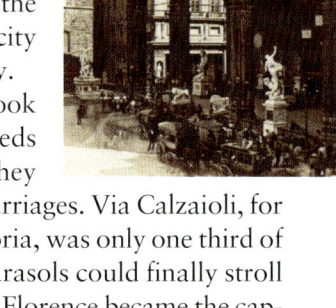

small squares with children at play, mothers sewing on the stairways of their houses—these images belonged to a city still quite close in time and nonetheless light years away.

The works that changed the face of Florence—the book explained—were undertaken to address a series of needs common to many great European cities of the day. They started by widening the streets to allow the passage of carriages. Via Calzaioli, for example, running from the Duomo to Piazza della Signoria, was only one third of its present size—width, I mean. The ladies with their parasols could finally stroll down it without tripping over their wide skirts. In 1865, Florence became the capital of Italy. It was an opportunity to expand the city with new neighbourhoods, and to lay the tree-lined avenues that surround the city centre: the so-called 'ring road,' that becomes a driver's nightmare every day come rush hour. To make way for the new streets, the ancient city walls were levelled—left standing, they

would have divided the old centre from the new areas under construction. The city gates, on the other hand, were left intact: isolated in the middle of new squares and stripped of their original function, they stand as mere monuments. At the end of the 19th century, many Italian cities were hit with cholera, a disease that swept through the more degraded neighbourhoods with particular ferocity. It was thus decided to level the medieval blocks that once flanked the Old Market—the area where the ancient Roman forum had stood. It was replaced with new, wider streets and modern buildings with offices, department stores, cinemas and cafes: Piazza della Repubblica and surroundings. It was a fairly brutal intervention. In one fell stroke, entire city blocks, churches, picturesque squares beloved by English residents and tourists—all wiped out… The families who had lived in the area were moved into large complexes in the suburbs. In that same area between the Old Market and the baptistery, the ghetto used to stand—the ancient Jewish quarter.

The drastic changes, Philip read on, were celebrated with a grand new arch in Piazza della Repubblica, where a plaque reads: *After centuries of squalor, the ancient city centre has been given new life.*

EPILOGUE

Back at home, Philip and his uncle parted ways. The archaeologist would spend his days in the library—"where it's cooler"—while his nephew barraged his relatives with stories about the wonders of Tuscany. Ignorant of all things having to do with walls, fortifications and defence strategy, the poor folks succumbed without great resistance. Not counting the vast sums that Philip requested for the acquisition of catalogues and art books, traditionally costly items.

Tearing himself away from his massive volumes on Brunelleschi and Paolo Uccello, Philip cast a sceptic glance over the drawings and sketches that lay scattered on his father's table—the project for a new shopping mall.

'The world's never gonna get a dome out of this family,' he muttered.

One day, studying a photo of the Dome, Philip read the words Vasari had written about his myth: *There are men whom nature has made small and insignificant, but who are so fiercely consumed by emotion and ambition that they know no peace unless they are grappling with difficult or indeed almost impossible tasks, and achieving astonishing results. These men enhance and distinguish whatever they happen to take up, no matter how commonplace or worthless it may seem.*

"Dinner's ready!" his mother yelled.

Lost in thought, Philip closed the book and went into the bathroom to wash his hands. Looking at himself in the mirror, he thought:

"I'm not so tall: maybe there's still hope after all."

His little sister raced down the stairs, screaming at the top of her lungs: "Mummy, Mummy! Philip's washing his hands with the toothpaste!"

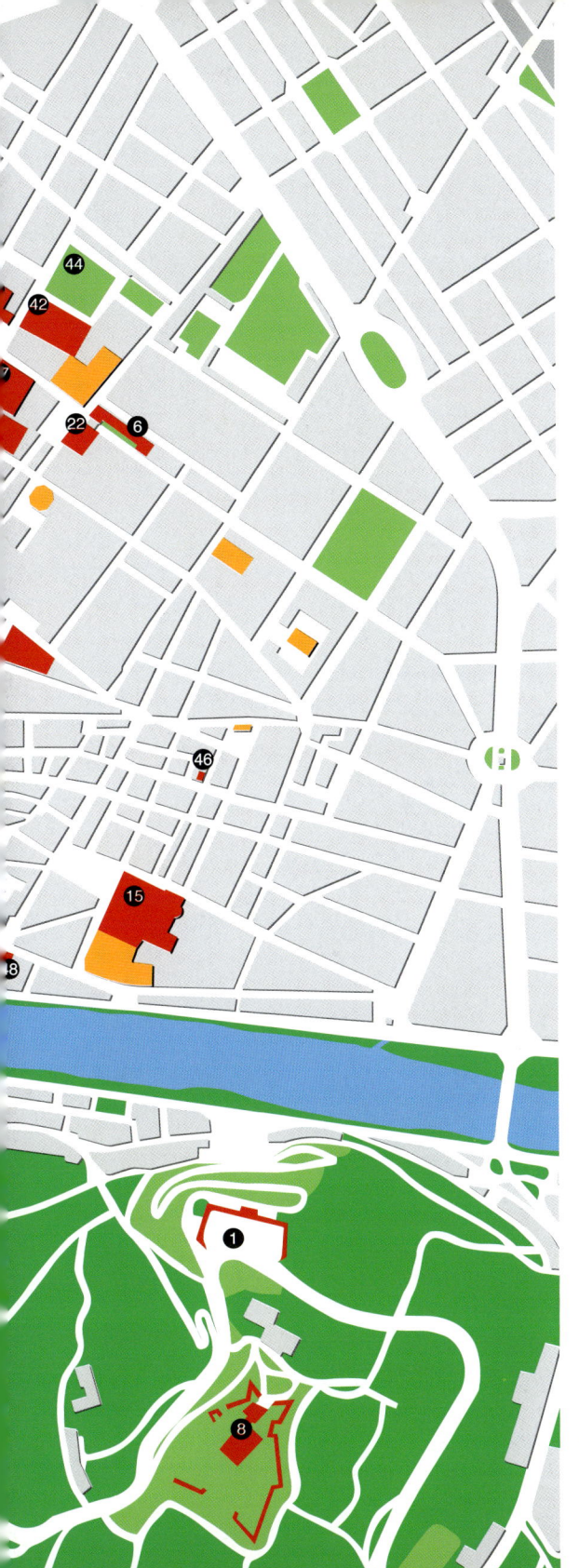

1 Piazzale Michelangelo
2 Battistero di San Giovanni
3 Campanile di Giotto
4 Cattedrale di Santa Maria del Fiore
5 Museo dell'Opera del Duomo
6 Museo Archeologico Nazionale
7 Palazzo Davanzati
8 San Miniato al Monte
9 Forte di Belvedere
10 Tribunale di Mercatanzia
11 Loggia dei Lanzi
12 Palazzo Vecchio
13 Porcellino
14 Orsanmichele
15 Santa Croce
16 Santa Maria Novella
17 Santa Trinita
18 Mercato Centrale
19 San Lorenzo
20 Cappelle Medicee
21 Museo dell'Opificio delle Pietre Dure
22 Spedale degli Innocenti
23 Palazzo Medici-Riccardi
24 Museo Nazionale del Bargello
25 Museo Stibbert
26 San Marco
27 Galleria dell'Accademia
28 Museo di Storia della Scienza
29 Galleria degli Uffizi
30 Corridoio Vasariano
31 Santa Felicita
32 Giardino di Boboli
33 Ponte Vecchio
34 Ponte a Santa Trinita
35 Ponte alla Carraia
36 Museo di Storia Naturale "La Specola"
37 Santo Spirito
38 Cappella Brancacci
39 Palazzo Pitti

And also...

40 Badia Fiorentina
41 Stazione di Santa Maria Novella
42 Museo di Storia Naturale (other depts.)
43 Museo di Antropologia & Etnologia
44 Giardino dei Semplici
45 Casa di Dante
46 Casa Buonarroti
47 Museo Bardini
48 Museo della Fondazione Horne
49 Museo Marino Marini

In this section the names of places are left in Italian—should make them easier to find!

ANALYTICAL INDEX

NAMES, PLACES, WORKS OF ART, NOTABILIA & WHATNOT

Abundance by Giambologna & Tacca 171
Academy Awards 92
Accademia delle Arti del Disegno 26
— Gallery 43, 131, 133–5
Achilles 50
Acuto, Giovanni (Sir John Hawkwood, *c.* 1320–94) 30; fresco by Uccello 30
Adam 24, 25, 186
Adoration of the Magi by Botticelli 162
— by Gentile 149–51
— by Leonardo 163
Adriatic Sea 145
Aeneid by Virgil 100
aerobics 15
Aeschylus (525–456 BC) 100
Agony & the Ecstasy, The by Reed 135
alabaster 62
Alberti, Leon Battista (1404–72) 34, 88, 93, 105
Alchemist's Laboratory by Stradano 78
alchemy 77, 107, 200
Alessandro de' Medici, duke of Florence (1511–37) 76, 117
Alexandria of Egypt 140
Alfieri, Vittorio (1749–1803) 88
Alighieri, Dante (1265–1321) 22, 68, 137, 138
Almagest by Ptolemy 140
America 107, 108, 136
Amerigo Vespucci Airport 12, 203
Amiatinus, Codex 100
Ammannati, Bartolomeo (1511–92) 71, 77, 173
—'s Courtyard 173–4
anatomical models 183
Ancient Florentine Home, Museum of → Davanzati, Palazzo
Andrea del Castagno (*c.* 1421–57) 189
— Pisano (1290/5–1349) 27
Angel Gabriel by Pontormo 169
Angelico, Fra (fra Giovanni da Fiesole, *c.* 1395–1455) 128–31, 189
Anna Maria Luisa de' Medici (1667–1743) 117
Annunciation
by Fra Angelico 130–1
— by G. da Maiano 36

— by Leonardo 163–4
— by Martini 146–7
Anthropological Museum 36
Anubis 8
Apollo 192, 193, 194
—, Room of 194
Apopis 8
Apennine Range 11
Approbation of the Rule by Ghirlandaio 96–7
— by Giotto 89
Apuan Alps 60, 132
Aquarius 141
Arbia River 68
Arcetri 143
Archaeological Museum 14, 47–51
Arezzo 49
Aristotle (384–22 BC) 137–8
armadillo 126
armillary spheres 94, 136–7, 141
armours 126–7
Arno River 10–12, 36, 63, 124, 132, 144, 166, 167, 175–80, 185
Arnolfo di Cambio (*c.* 1245–1302) 25, 26, 32, 41, 68, 81, 87
Arte della Lana, Palazzo dell' 83
Assayer* by Galileo 141–2
Assisi 89
astrolabes 136
Athena 49, 73, 157, 193
Atlantis 7, 10
Audience Room 79
Aulus Metellus 50
Australia 79
Aventine Hill 72
Avignon 147

Bacchino 170
backgammon 122
Bandinelli, Baccio (1488–1560) 72
baptism 19
— *of Christ* by Tino di Camaino 121
Baptistery → San Giovanni, Baptistery of
Barbadori-Capponi Chapel 168–9
barbarians 18, 63, 66
Barberini, Maffeo Cardinal (Urban VIII, Pope, 1568–1644) 142
Bardi Chapel 88–90
— di Vernio Chapel 90

bargello 56
— National Museum 42, 83, 118–23, 134
— Palace 56, 68, 118–20, 158
bartisans 64
Bartolomeo, Fra (Baccio della Porta, 1472/5–1517) 128
bastions & ramparts 65, 171
Batman 71
Battle of San Romano by Uccello 154–6
Bavaria, dukes of 53
Bellerophon 49
Bellosguardo 13
Belvedere, Fort 63–5, 171
Ben Hur by Wyler 92
Bernardo Bandini Baroncelli by Leonardo 37
Bethlehem 149
Bia de' Medici by Bronzino 166–7
Biancone → Neptune's Fountain
Bible 62, 96, 100, 140
Bigallo Confraternity 109
Birth of Venus by Botticelli 157, 158–9
Black Corsair 126
— Death → plague
Blade Runner by Scott 109
Blessed Umiltà Altarpiece by Lorenzetti 148
Boboli Gardens 169–73, 192, 197; Amphitheatre 173; Isolotto 172; obelisk 173
Boccaccio, Giovanni (1313–75) 27
Bologna 137
Book of the Dead 10
Botticelli, Sandro (Alessandro Filipepi, 1445–1510) 144, 157–62, 164
Brancacci Chapel 145, 186–9
—, Felice (15th cent.) 186
Brescia 149
Bronzino (Agnolo di Cosimo Tori, 1503–72) 78, 166
Brunelleschi, Filippo (1377–1446) 28, 31, 32–5, 37, 41–2, 91, 94, 96, 98, 99, 100, 103, 105, 110–1, 112–3, 151, 175, 185, 205
—'s Dome (*Cupola*) 11, 19, 26, 32–5, 37–8, 41, 42; model 42; Lantern 34

Bruni, Leonardo (*c.* 1374–1444) 88
Brussels 171
Buonarroti, Michelangelo (1475–1564) 24, 43, 64, 72, 76, 87, 88, 99, 100, 102–3, 113, 132–5, 149, 159, 163, 164–5, 167, 169, 189, 199
Buontalenti, Bernardo (1536–1608) 25–6, 37, 41, 65, 167, 169–70, 173, 201
—'s Grotto 169–70
—, ice-cream flavour 37
burgonet 123
Burton, Richard (1925–84) 179
Buti, Lucrezia (15th cent.) 145
Bylivelt, Jacques (1550–1603) 201

cacciucco 107
Cacus 72
calidarium 17–8
Calimala → Guilds
Canova, Antonio (1757–1822) 193
cantoria → singing-gallery
Capitol 46
capoletti 58
Capricorn 62, 141, 194
Caracalla, Baths of 173
Caravaggio (Michelangelo Merisi, 1571/3–1610) 73
cardo 11–2, 46
Caro-Kann Defence (1. e4 c6) 18

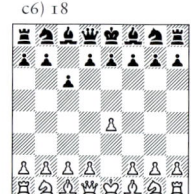

Carraia Bridge 181
Carrand Room 123
Carter, Howard (1874–1939) 8
Castagna Tower 56
Castello Sforzesco (Milan) 43
casting *à cire perdue* 73
castrum 11–2, 46
Catena, Carta della 12
Caterina de' Medici (1519–89) 118, 198, 199

208

TABLE OF CONTENTS

NOTES

March 2019
Print: Grafiche Martinelli, Bagno a Ripoli (Florence)
Binding: Legatoria Giagnoni, Calenzano (Florence)